Felix Pastorius

Scales from Rhythm and Outer Space... aka Tetra Cocktails

All rights reserved. No part of this publication may be reproduced, distributed, or transmitted in any form or by any means, including photocopying, recording, or other electronic or mechanical methods, without the prior written permission of the author, Felix Pastorius.

Table of Ingredients	5
#1	6
#2 Symmetrical(#1)	10
#3	14
#4	18
#5	22
#6	26
#7	30
#8	34
#9	38
#10	42
#11	46
#12	50
#13	54
#14 Symmetrical(#2)	58
#15	62
#16	66
#17	70
#18	74
#19	78
#20	82
#21	86
#22 Symmetrical(#3)	90
#23	94
#24 Parallel(#1)	98
#25	102
#26	106
#27	110
#28	114
#29 Mixolydian(#9#11)	118
#30 Mixolydian(b9#11)	122
#31 Minor(Harmonic)	126
#32 Minor(Melodic)	130
#33 Symmetrical(#4)	134
#34 Major(Harmonic)	138
#35 Parallel(#2)	142
#36	146
#37	150
#38 Major	154

1. I wrote this book as a vehicle for exploration.
2. Technique is derived from tone and not injuring yourself.
3. Practicing slow and correct is always more productive than practicing fast and incorrect.
4. At least 50% of the time the most important note is the one you don't play.
5. Music is empathy.

Table of Ingredients

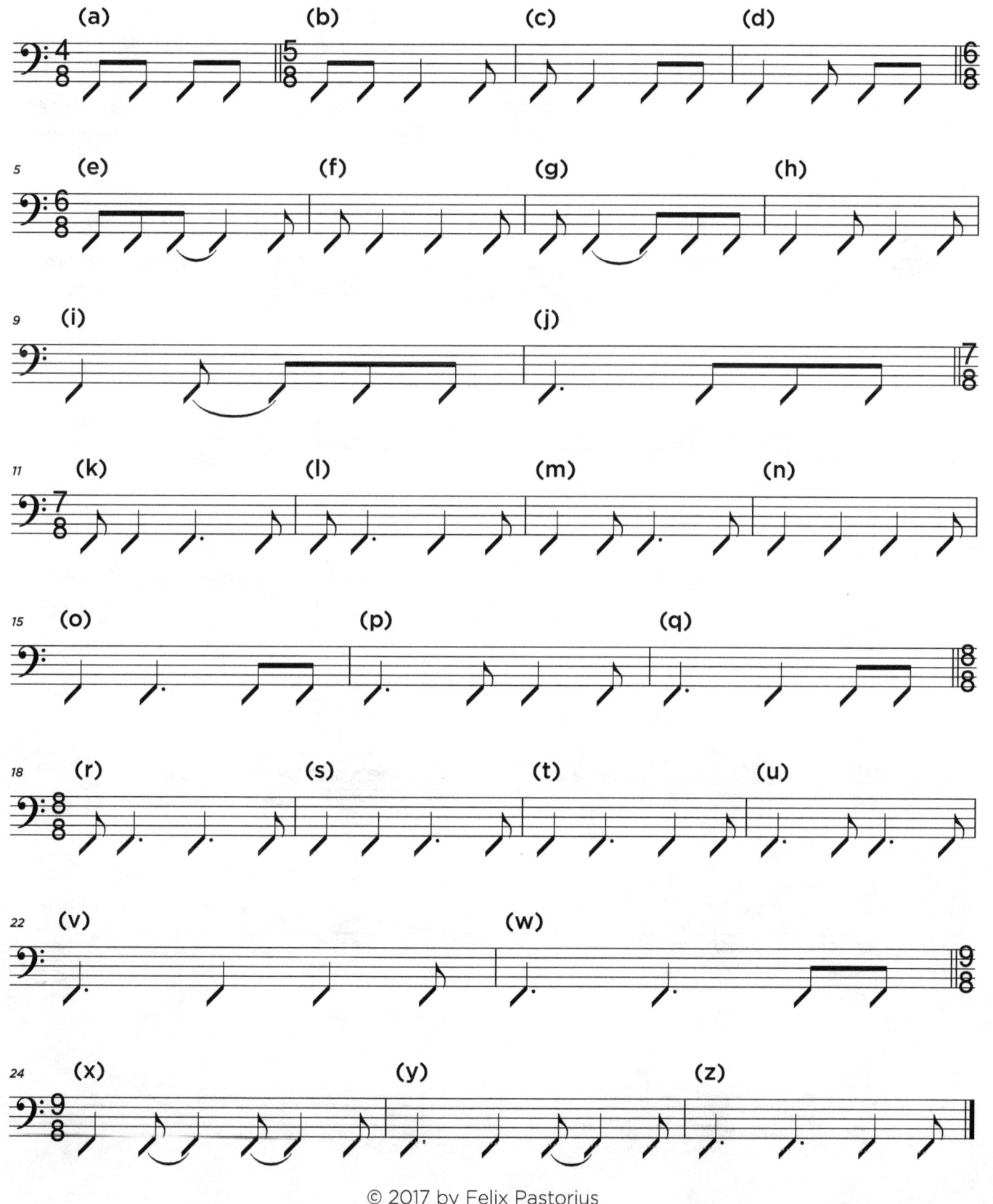

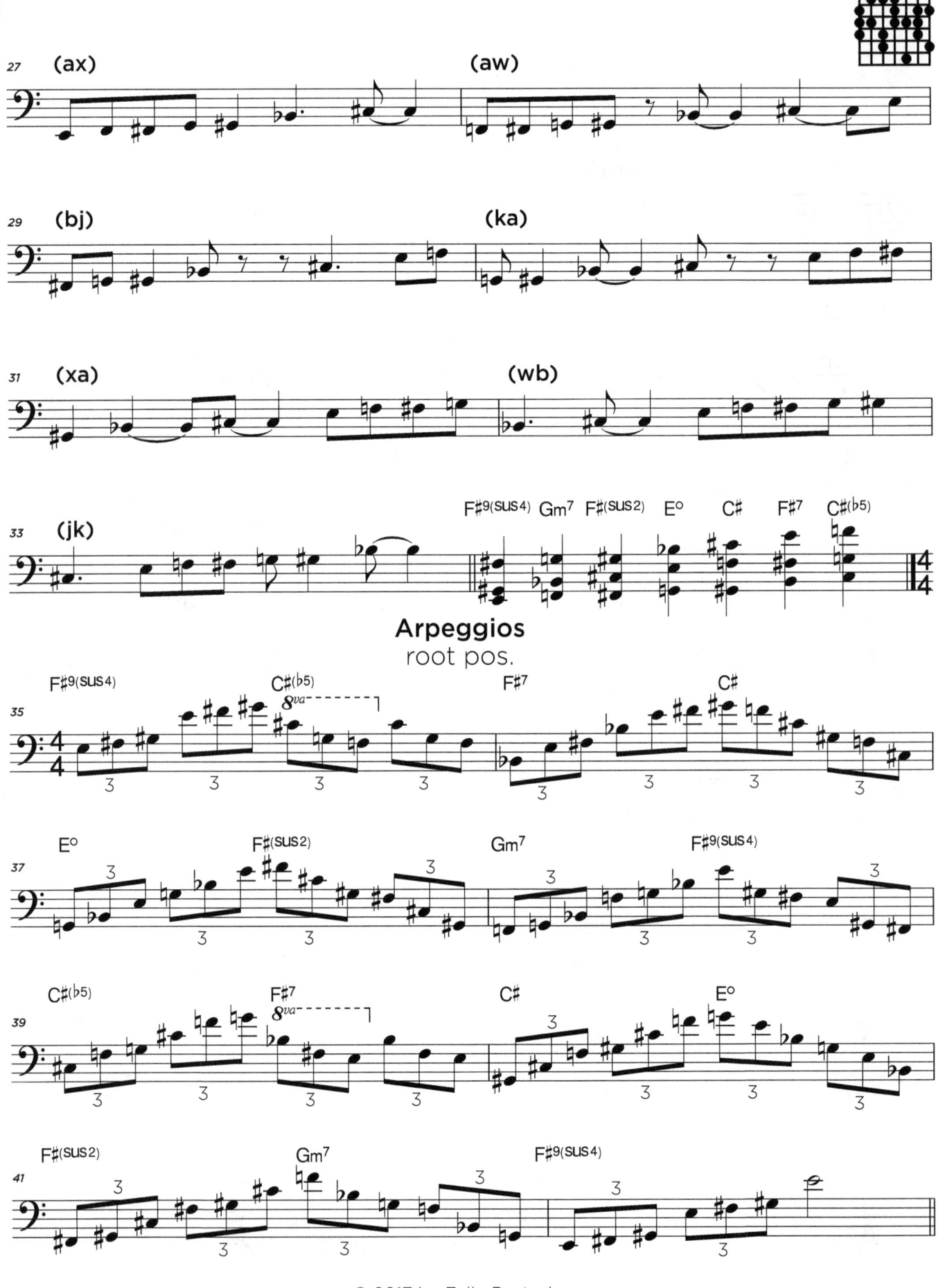

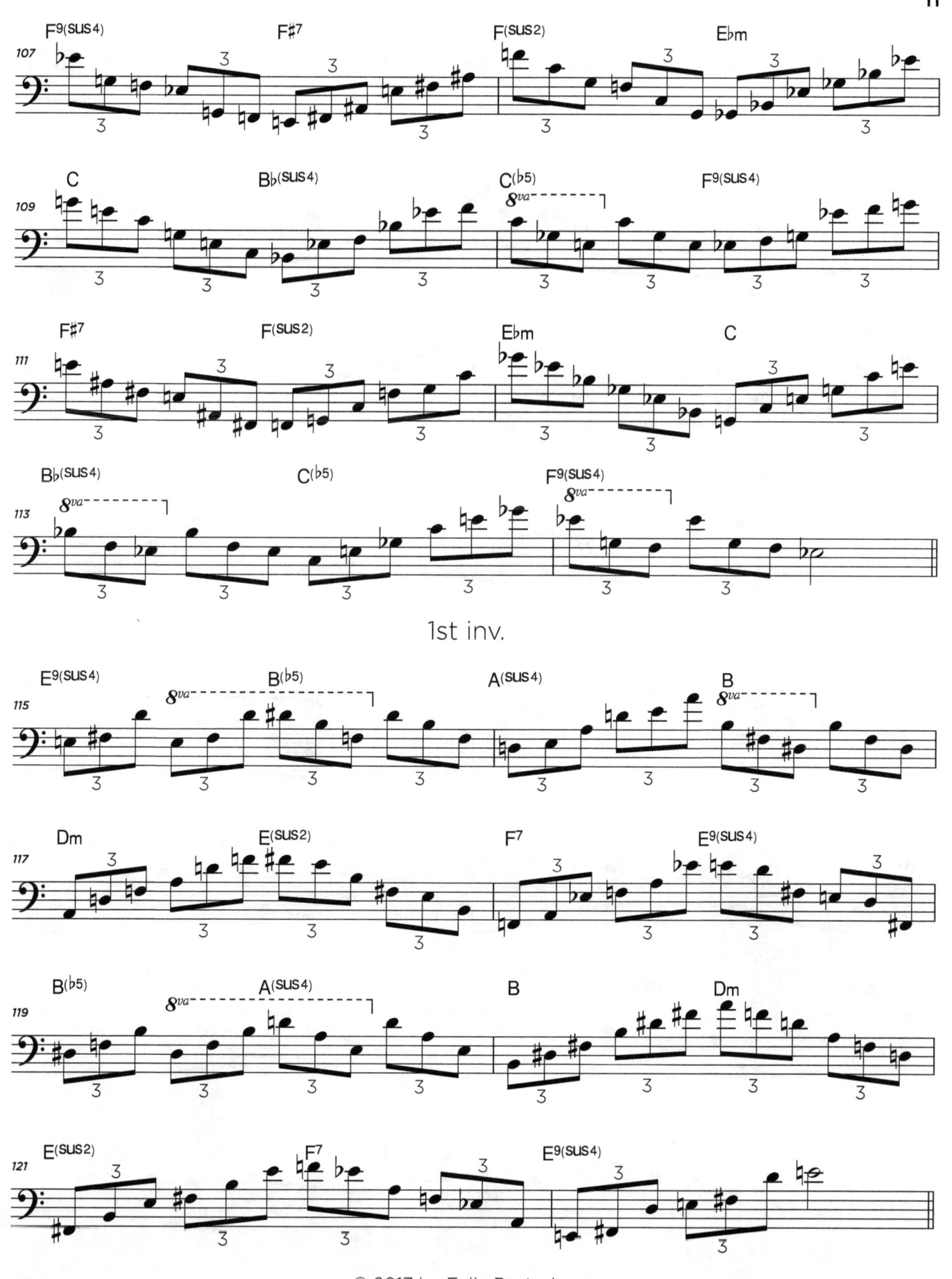

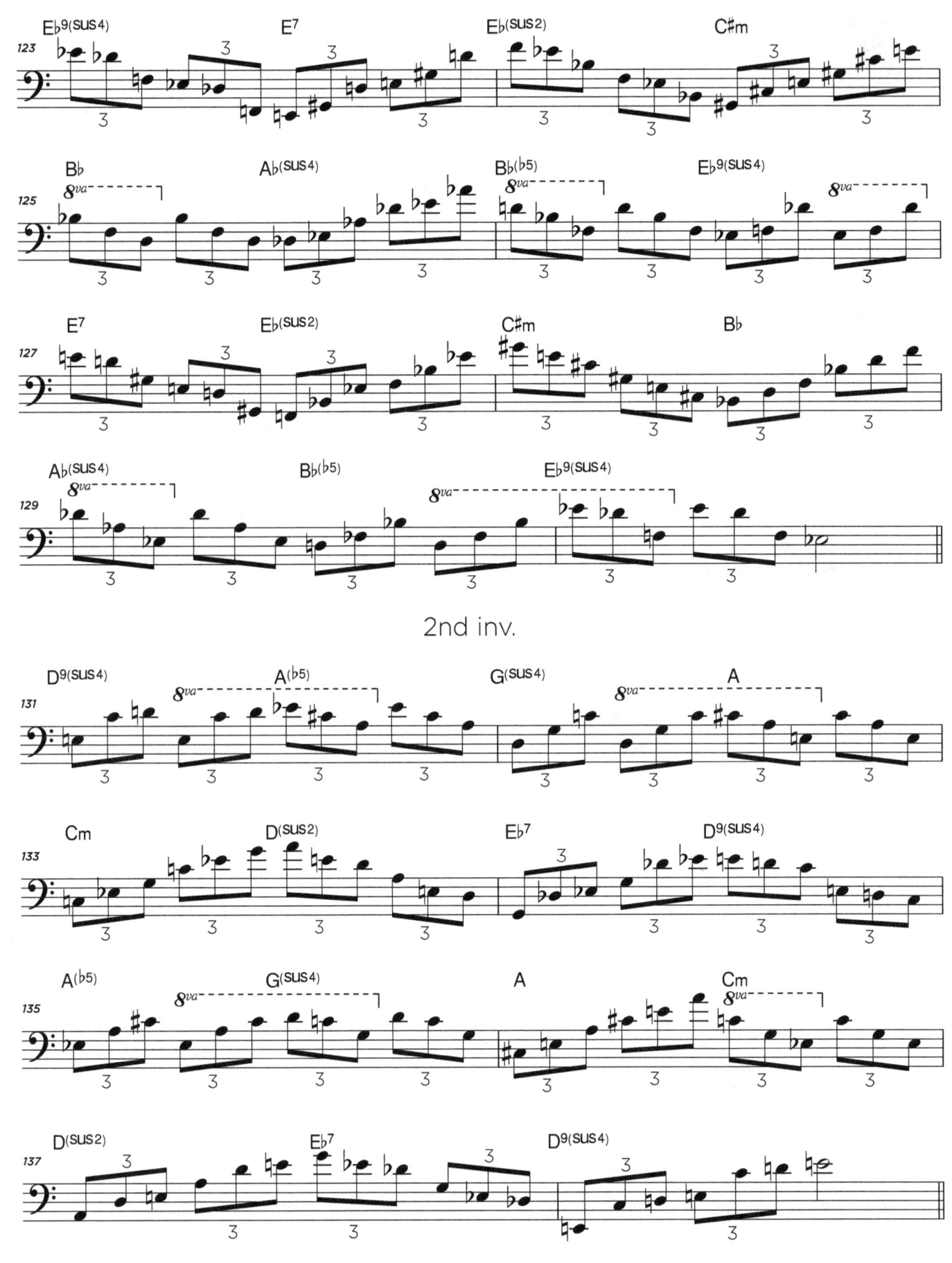

Voice Leading

© 2017 by Felix Pastorius

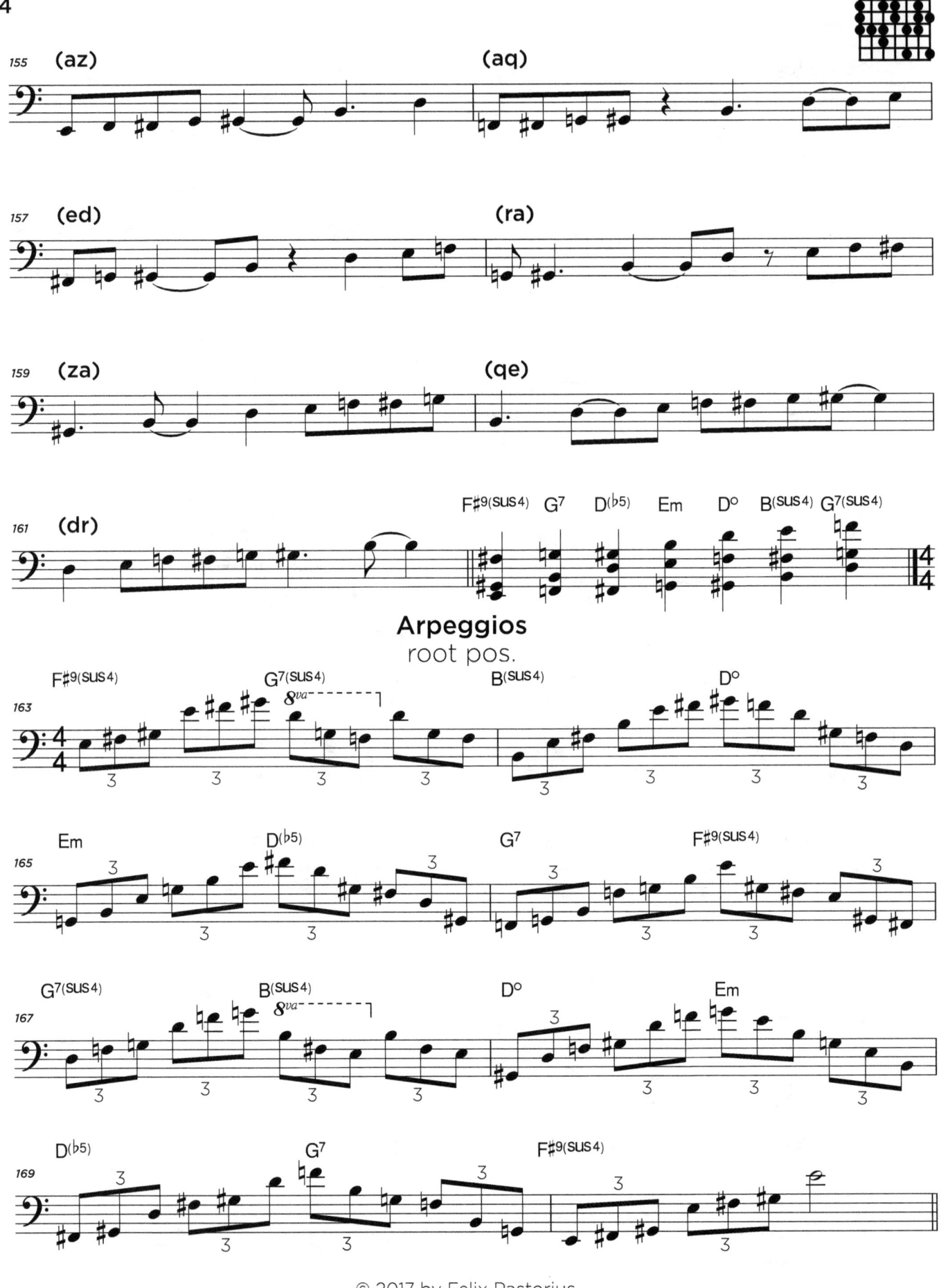

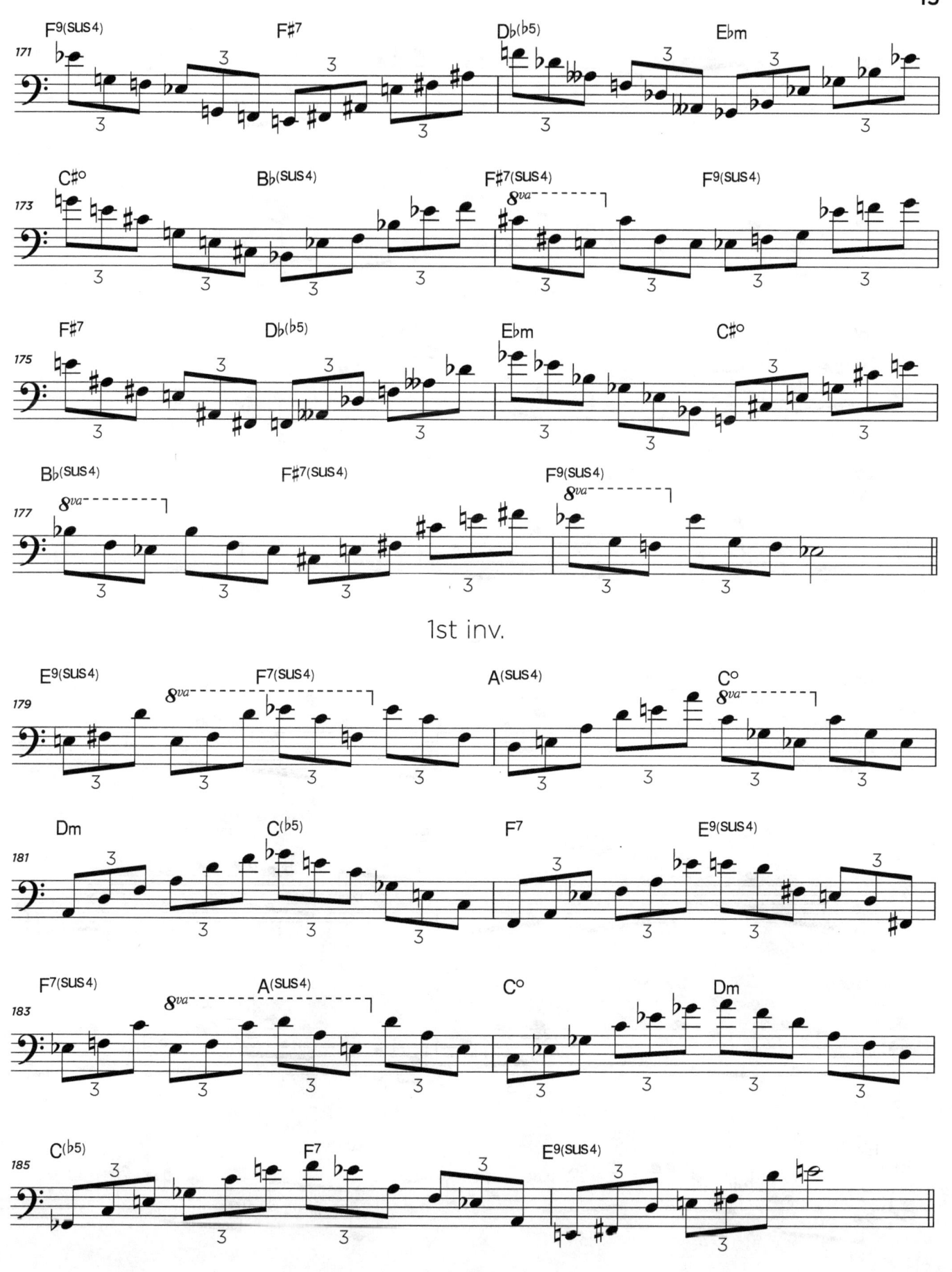

Voice Leading

© 2017 by Felix Pastorius

Voice Leading

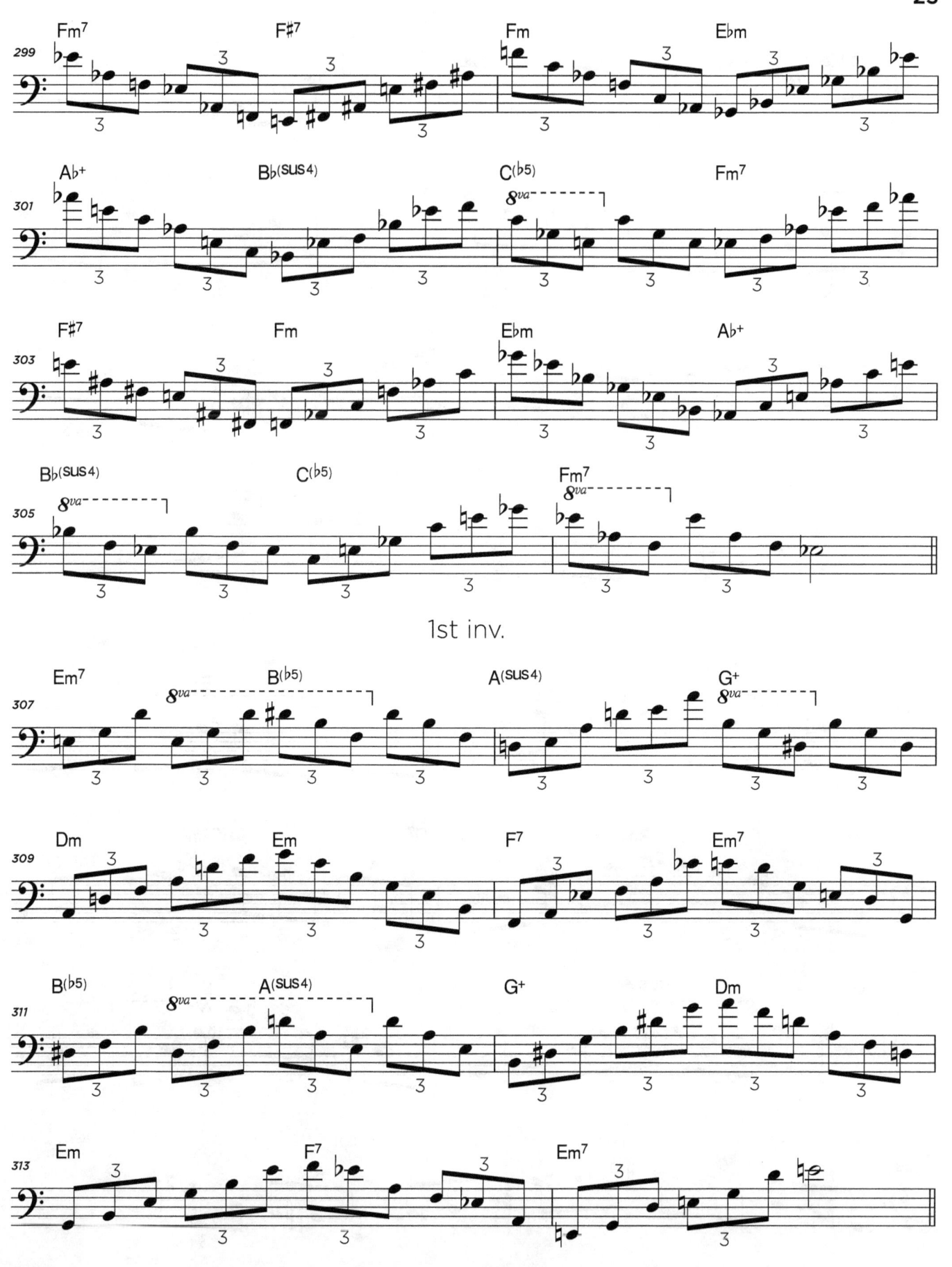

Voice Leading

© 2017 by Felix Pastorius

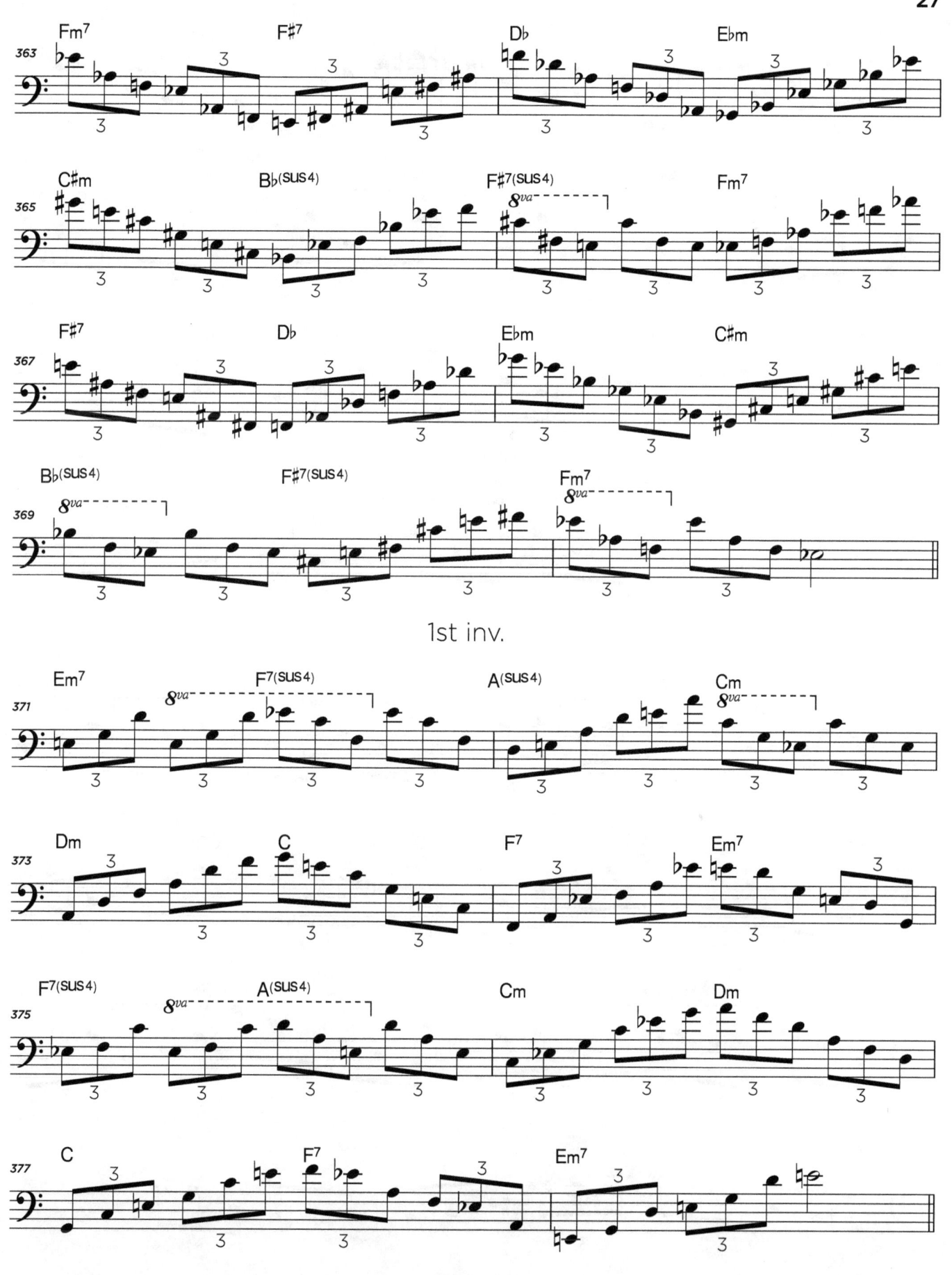

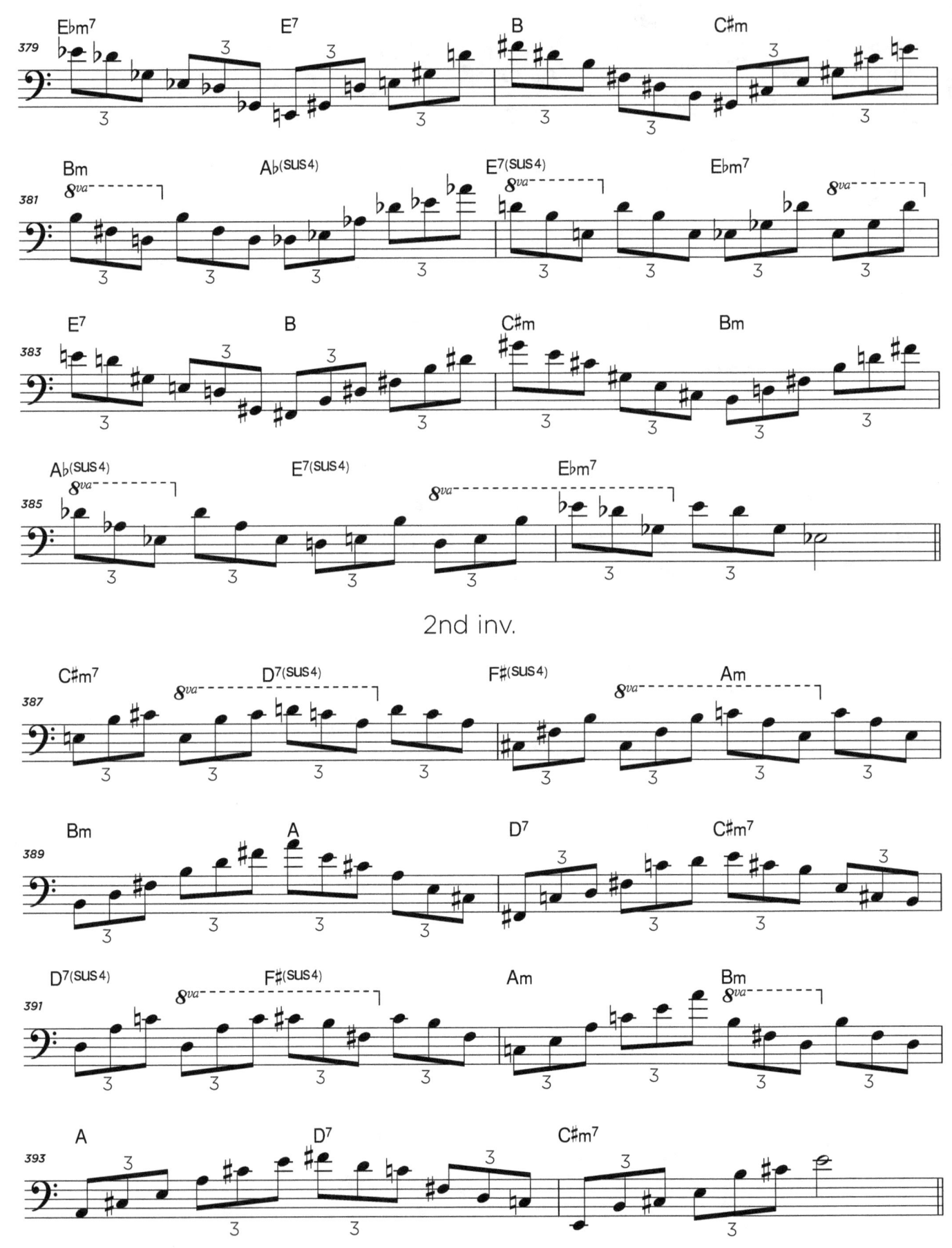

Voice Leading

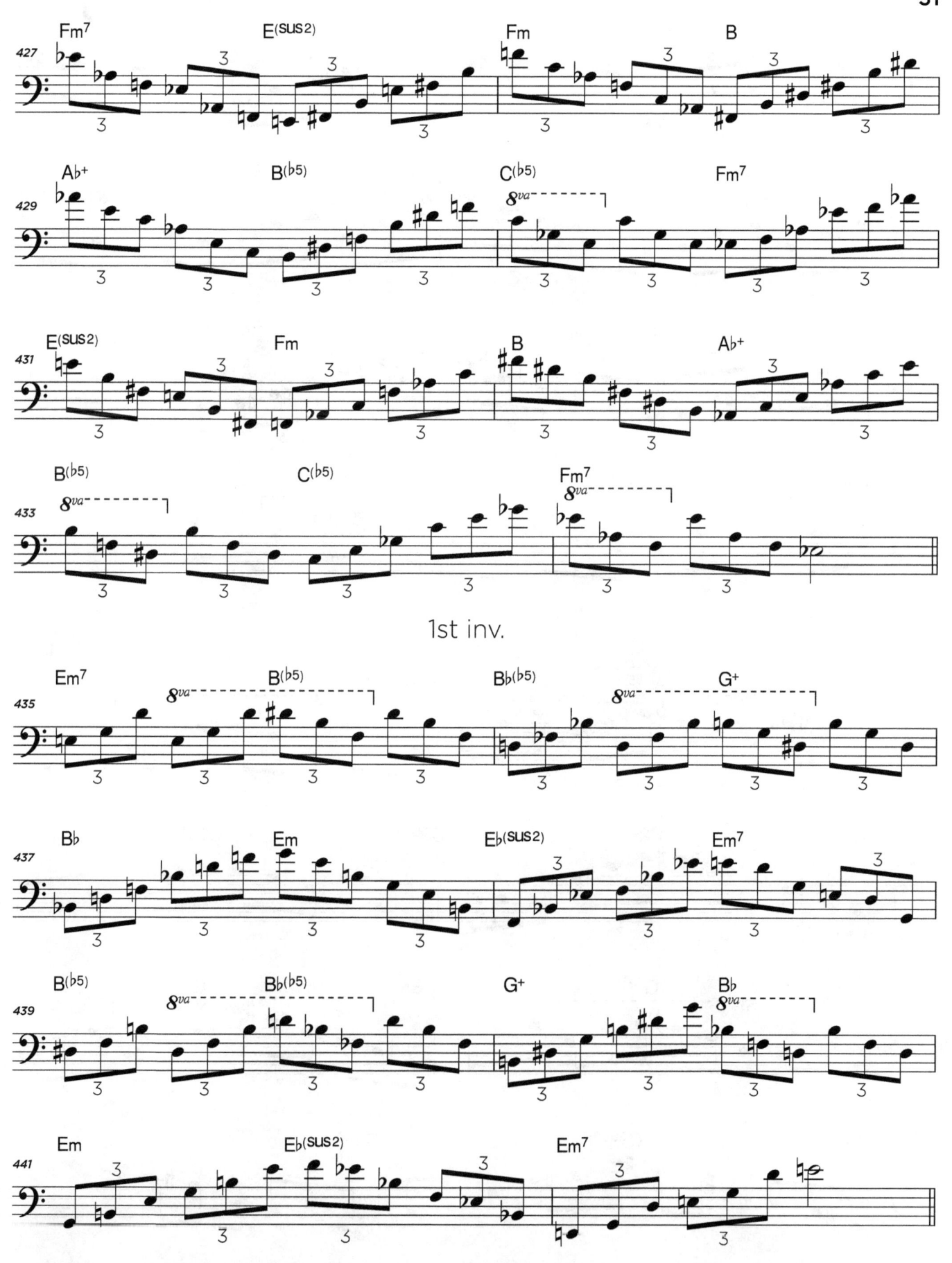

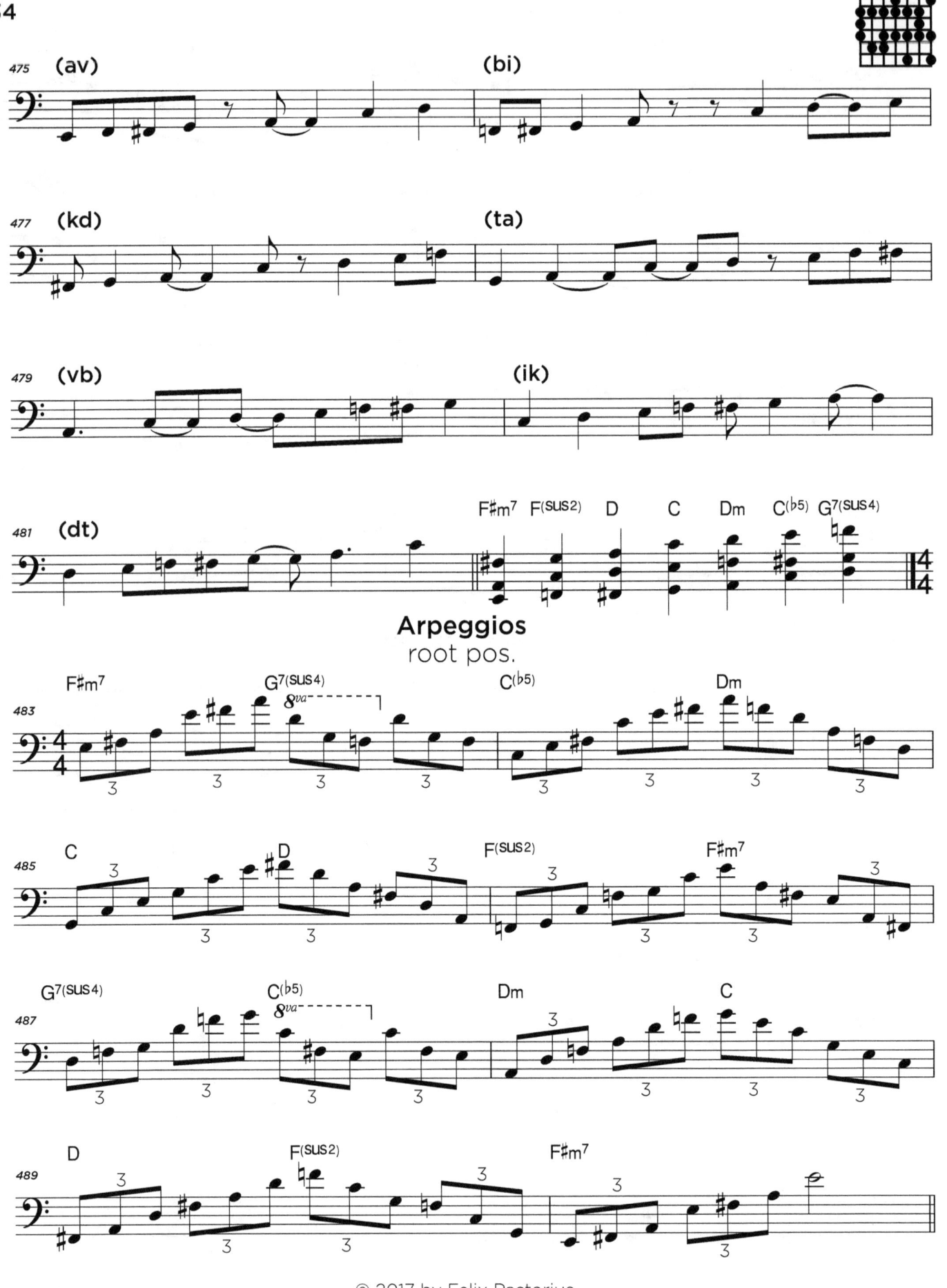

Voice Leading

#9

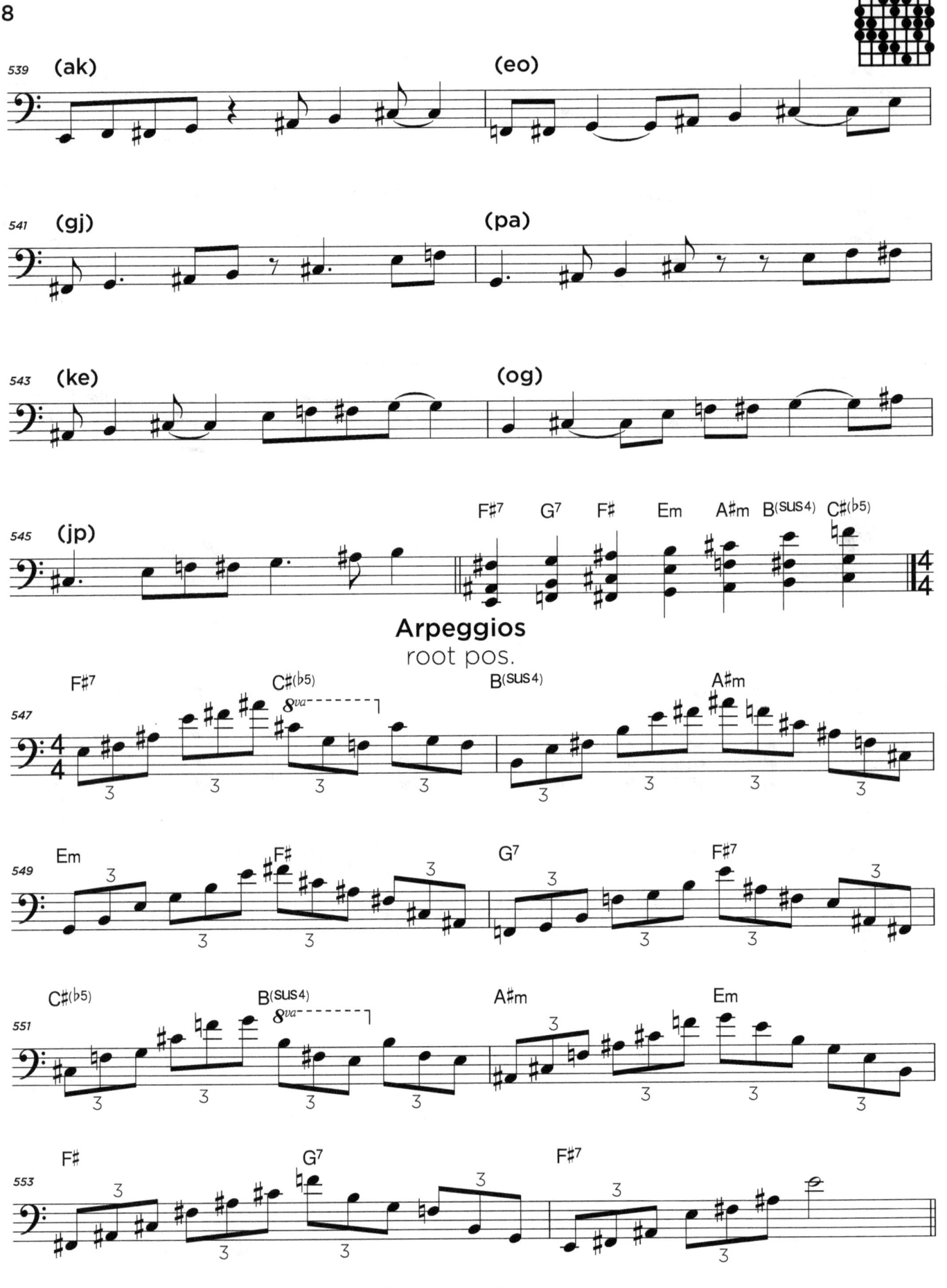

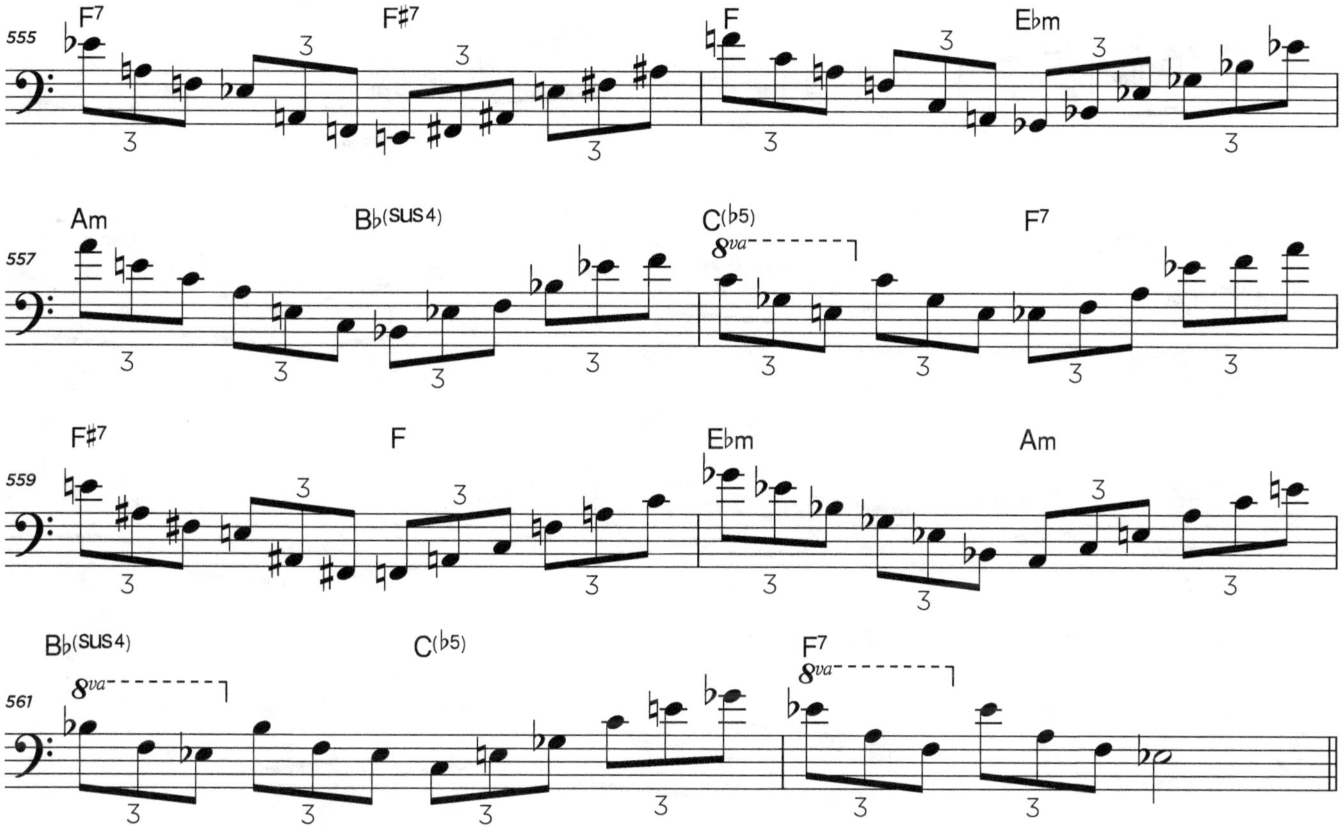
555
F7 F♯7 F E♭m
557
Am B♭(sus4) C(♭5) F7
559
F♯7 F E♭m Am
561
B♭(sus4) C(♭5) F7

1st inv.

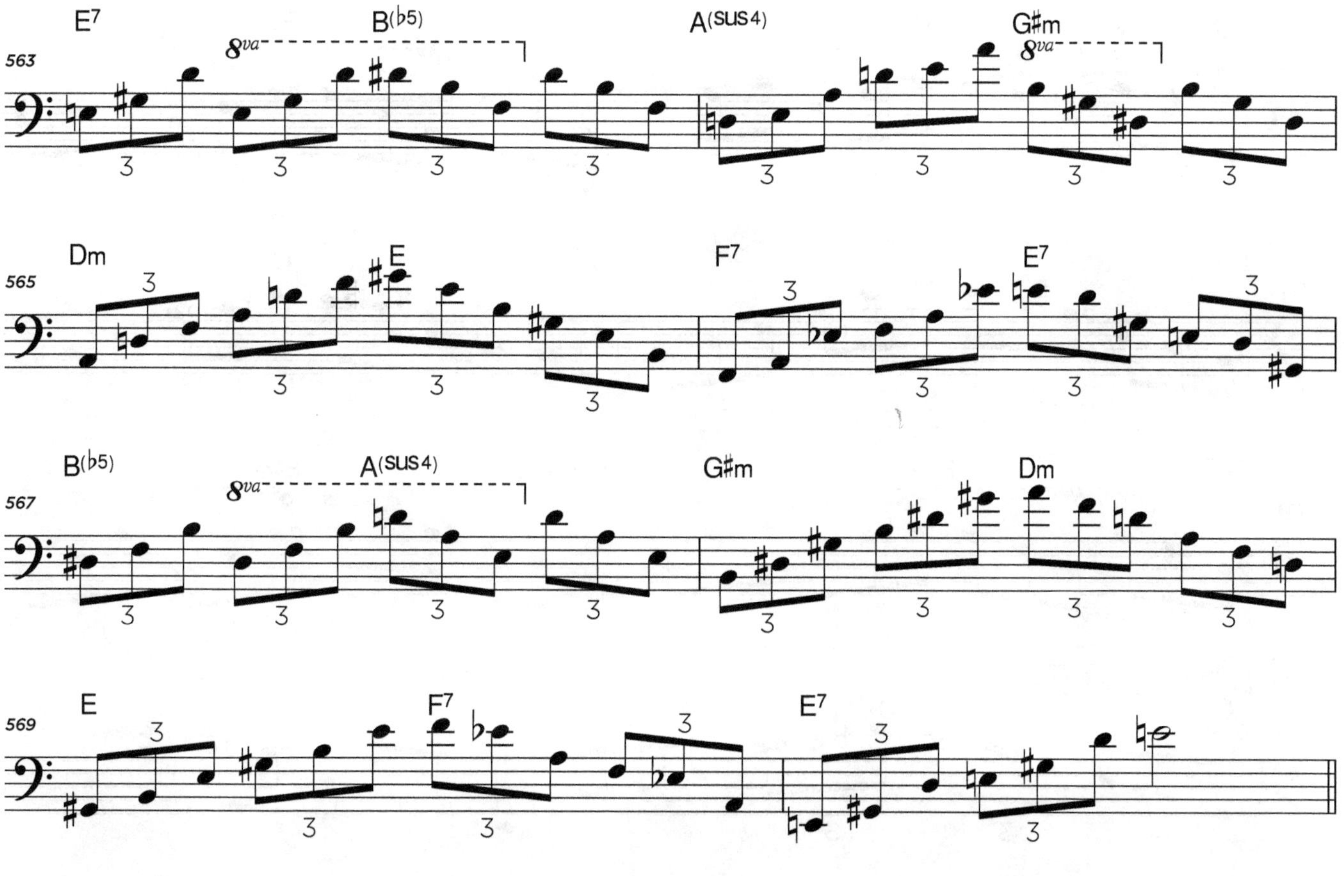
563
E7 B(♭5) A(sus4) G♯m
565
Dm E F7 E7
567
B(♭5) A(sus4) G♯m Dm
569
E F7 E7

571
Eb7
E7
Eb
C#m
573
Gm
Ab(sus4)
Bb(b5)
Eb7
575
E7
Eb
C#m
Gm
577
Ab(sus4)
Bb(b5)
Eb7

2nd inv.

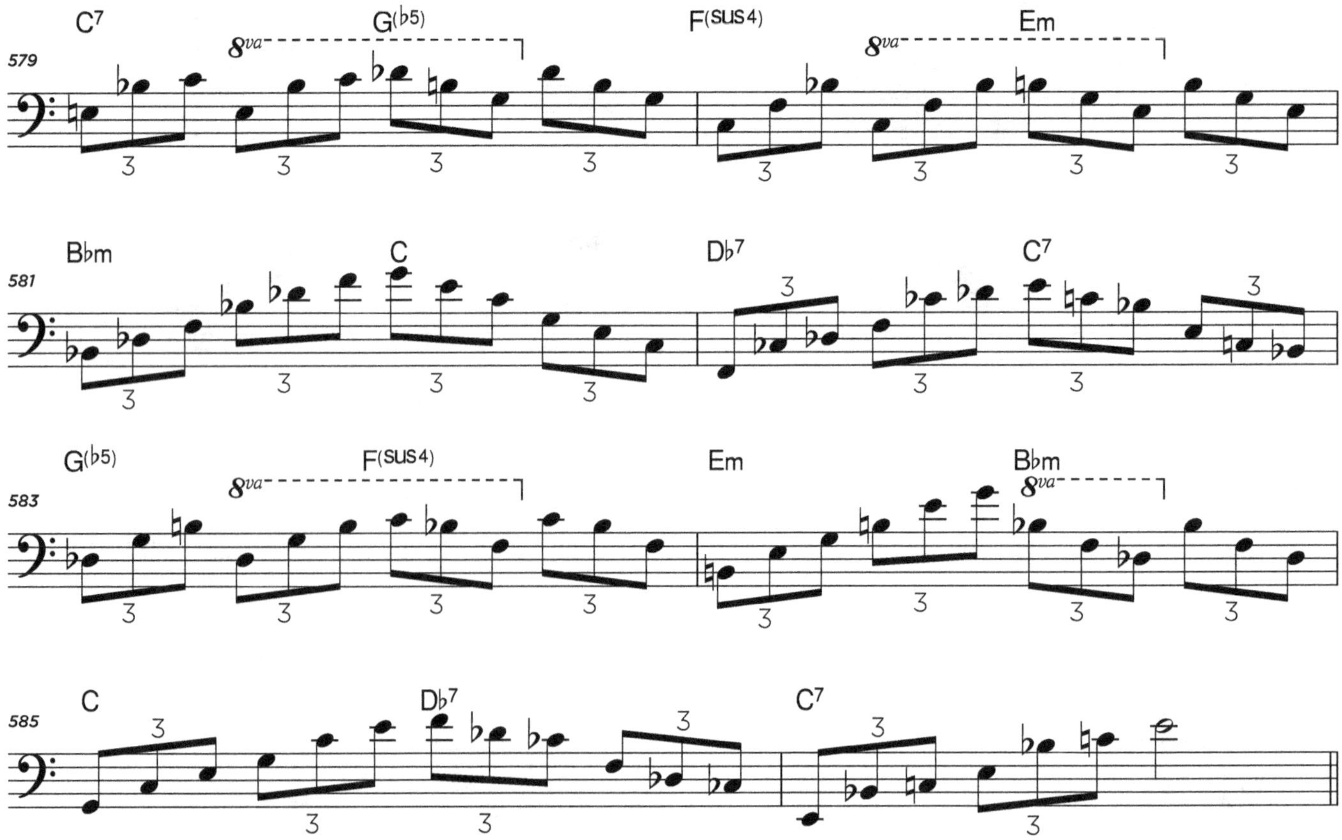
579
C7
G(b5)
F(sus4)
Em
581
Bbm
C
Db7
C7
583
G(b5)
F(sus4)
Em
Bbm
585
C
Db7
C7

Voice Leading

#10

619
F7
F♯7
F+
E♭m
621
A
B♭(SUS4)
F♯7(SUS4)
F7
623
F♯7
F+
E♭m
A
625
B♭(SUS4)
F♯7(SUS4)
F7

1st inv.

627
E7
F7(SUS4)
A(SUS4)
A♭
629
Dm
E+
F7
E7
631
F7(SUS4)
A(SUS4)
A♭
Dm
633
E+
F7
E7

635
E♭7 E7 E♭+ C♯m
637
G A♭(SUS4) E7(SUS4) E♭7
639
E7 E♭+ C♯m G
641
A♭(SUS4) E7(SUS4) E♭7

2nd inv.

643
C7 D♭7(SUS4) F(SUS4) E
645
B♭m C+ D♭7 C7
647
D♭7(SUS4) F(SUS4) E B♭m
649
C+ D♭7 C7

Voice Leading

#11

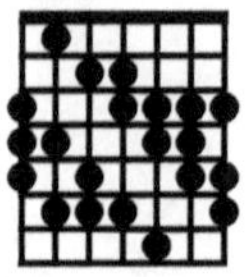

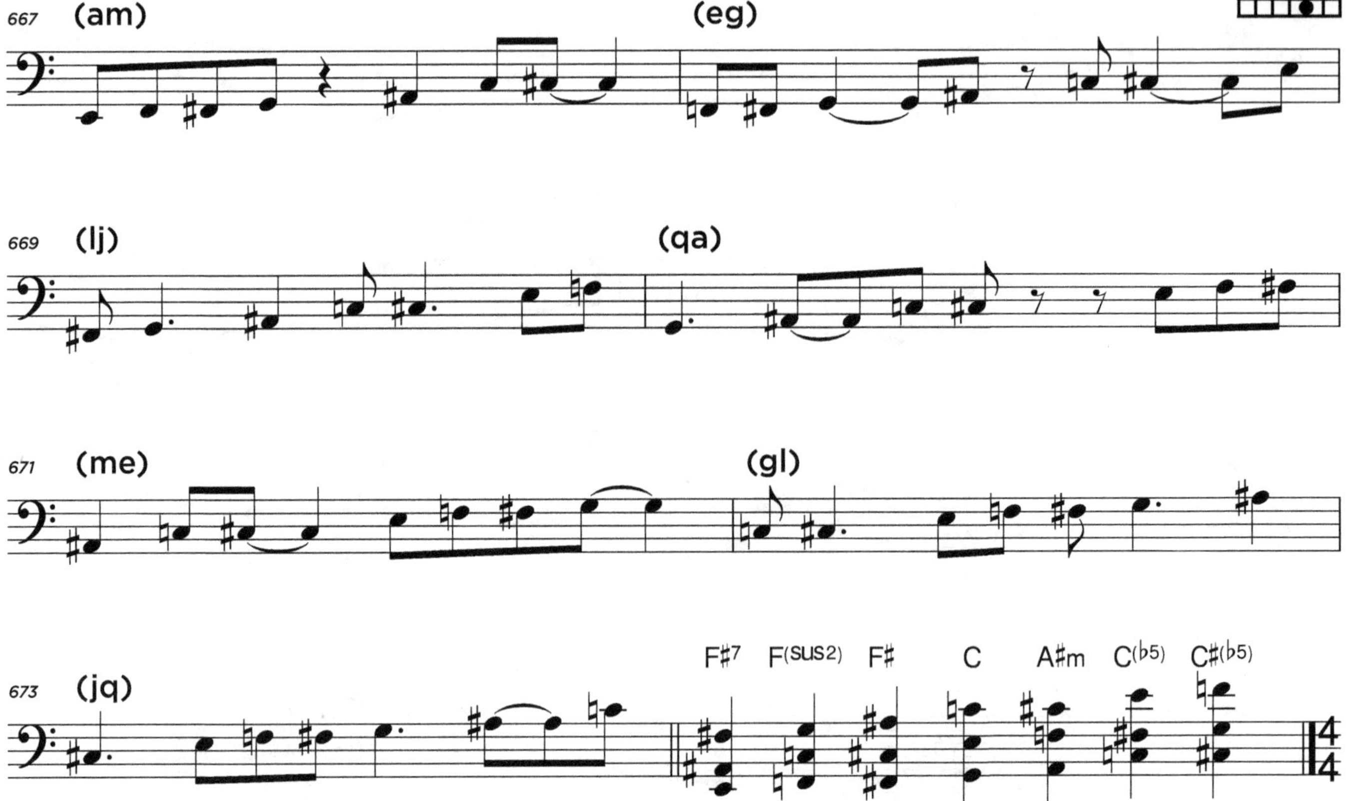

Arpeggios
root pos.

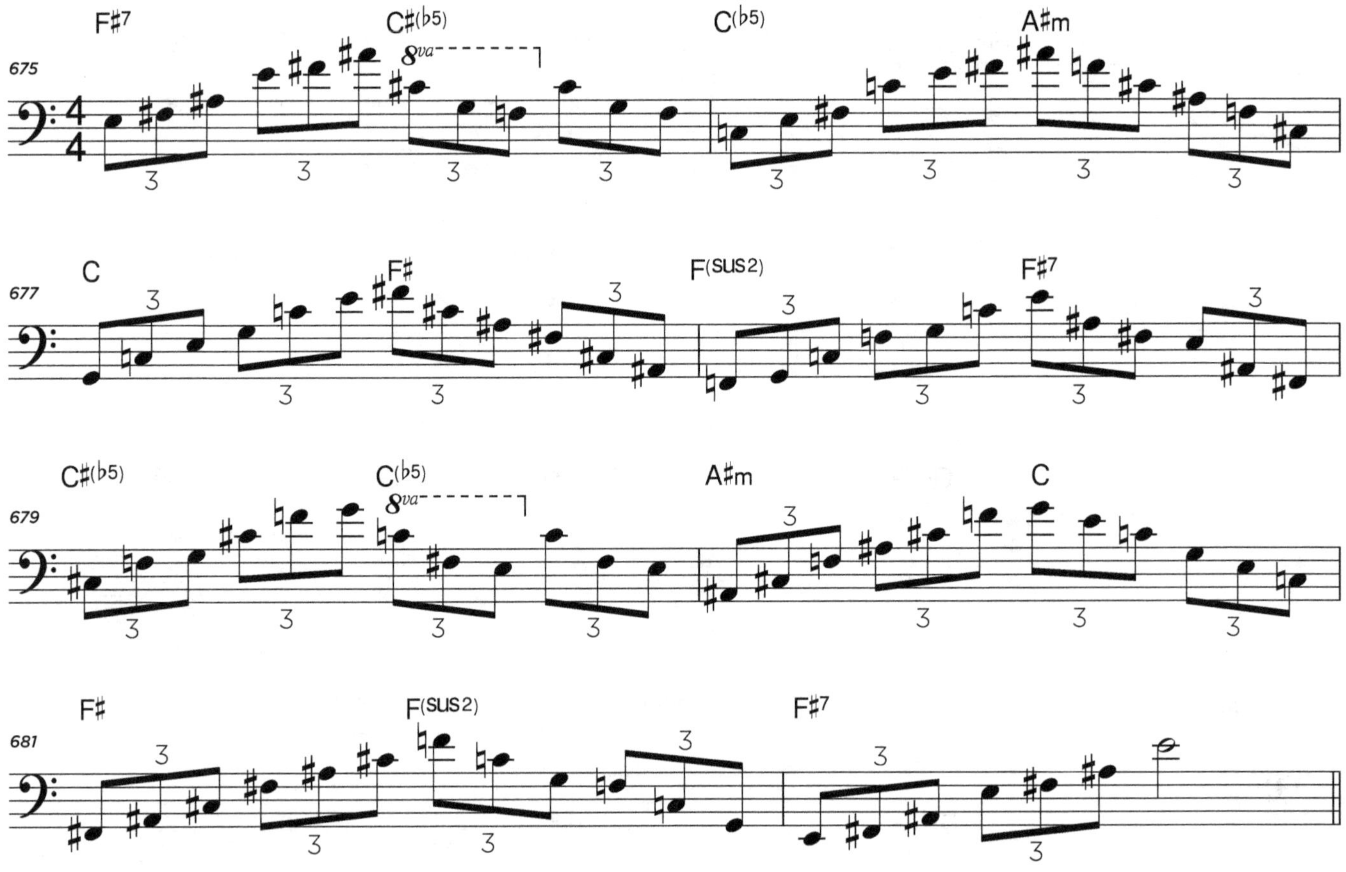

1st inv.

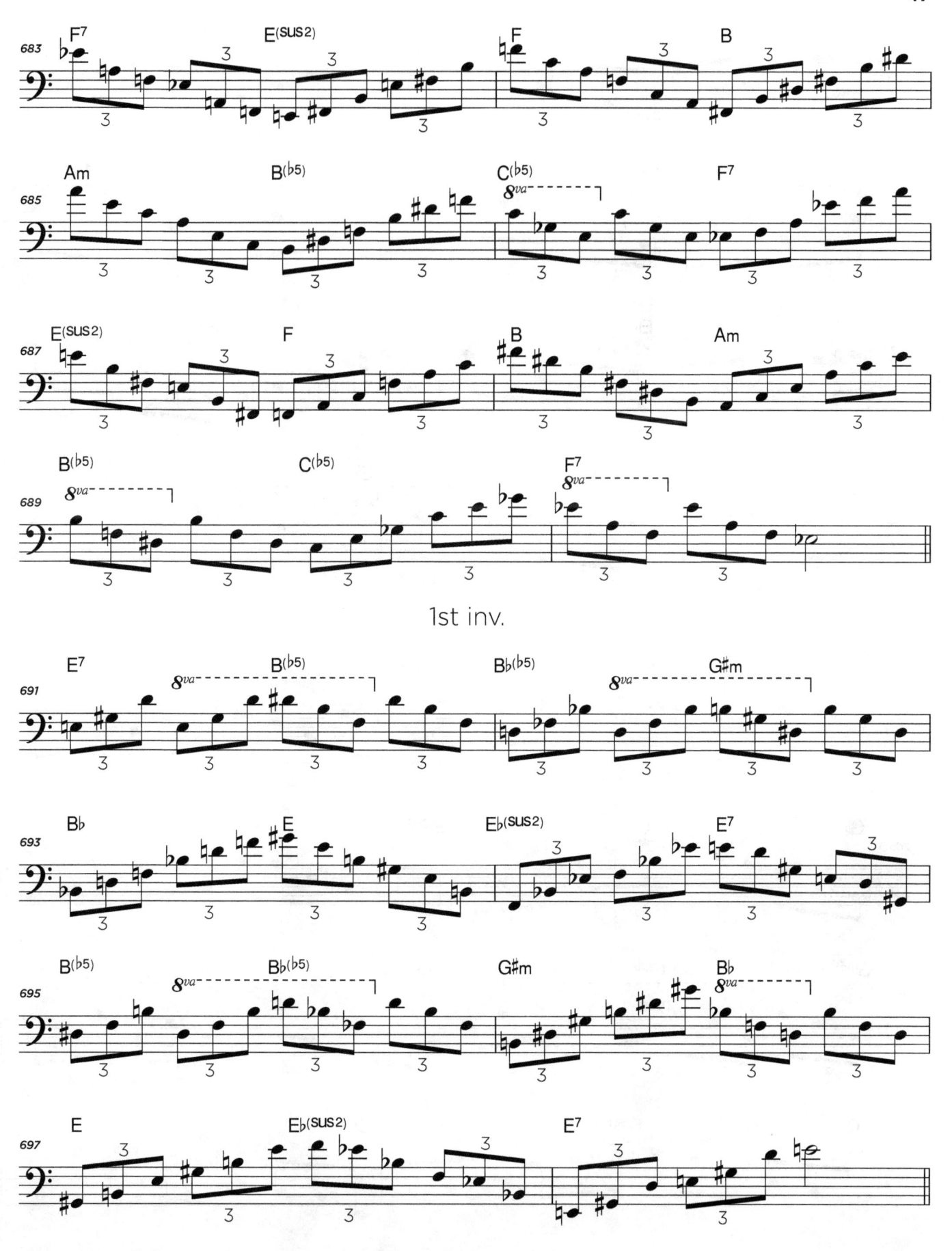

699
E♭7
D(sus2)
E♭
A
701
Gm
A(♭5)
B♭(♭5)
E♭7
703
D(sus2)
E♭
A
Gm
705
A(♭5)
B♭(♭5)
E♭7

2nd inv.

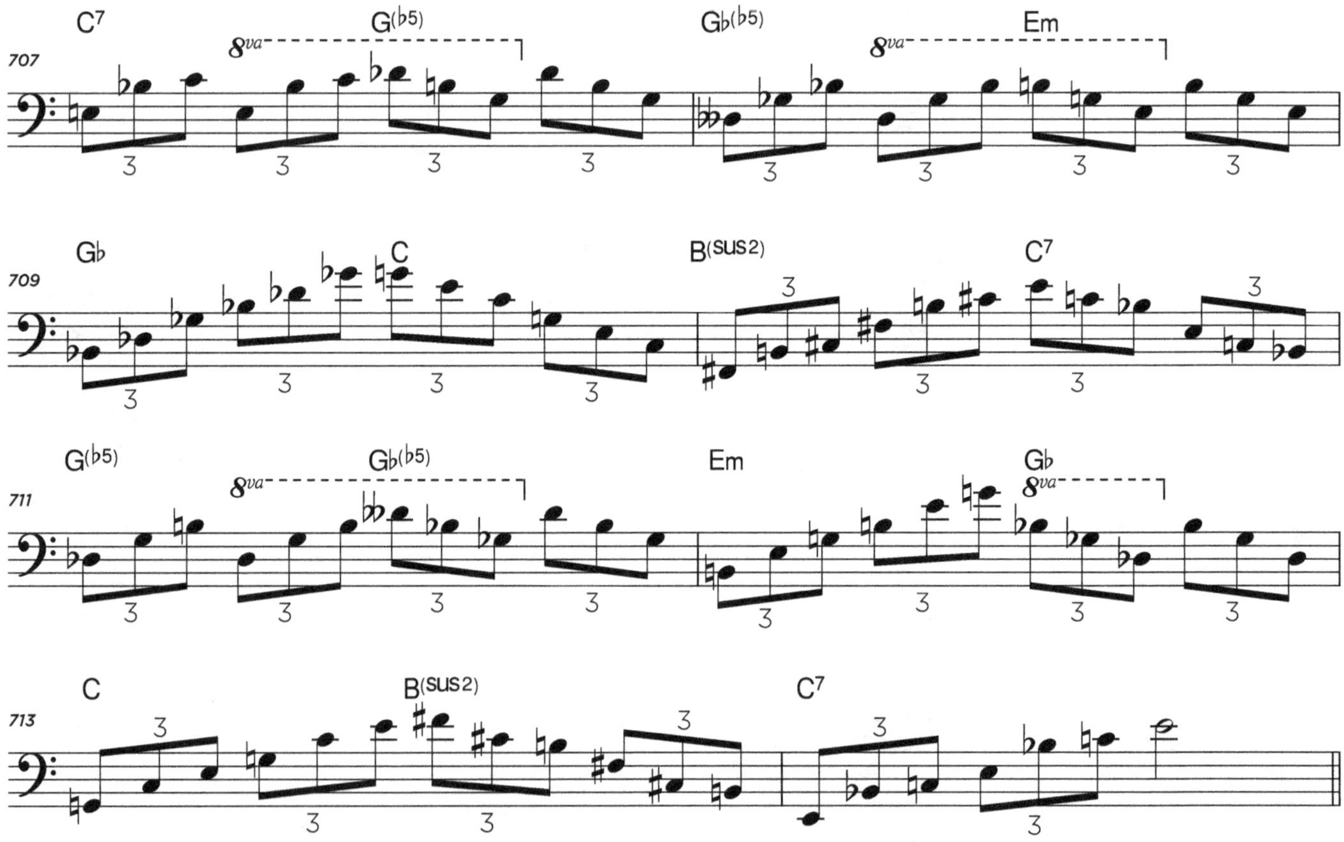
707
C7
G(♭5)
G♭(♭5)
Em
709
G♭
C
B(sus2)
C7
711
G(♭5)
G♭(♭5)
Em
G♭
713
C
B(sus2)
C7

Voice Leading

#12

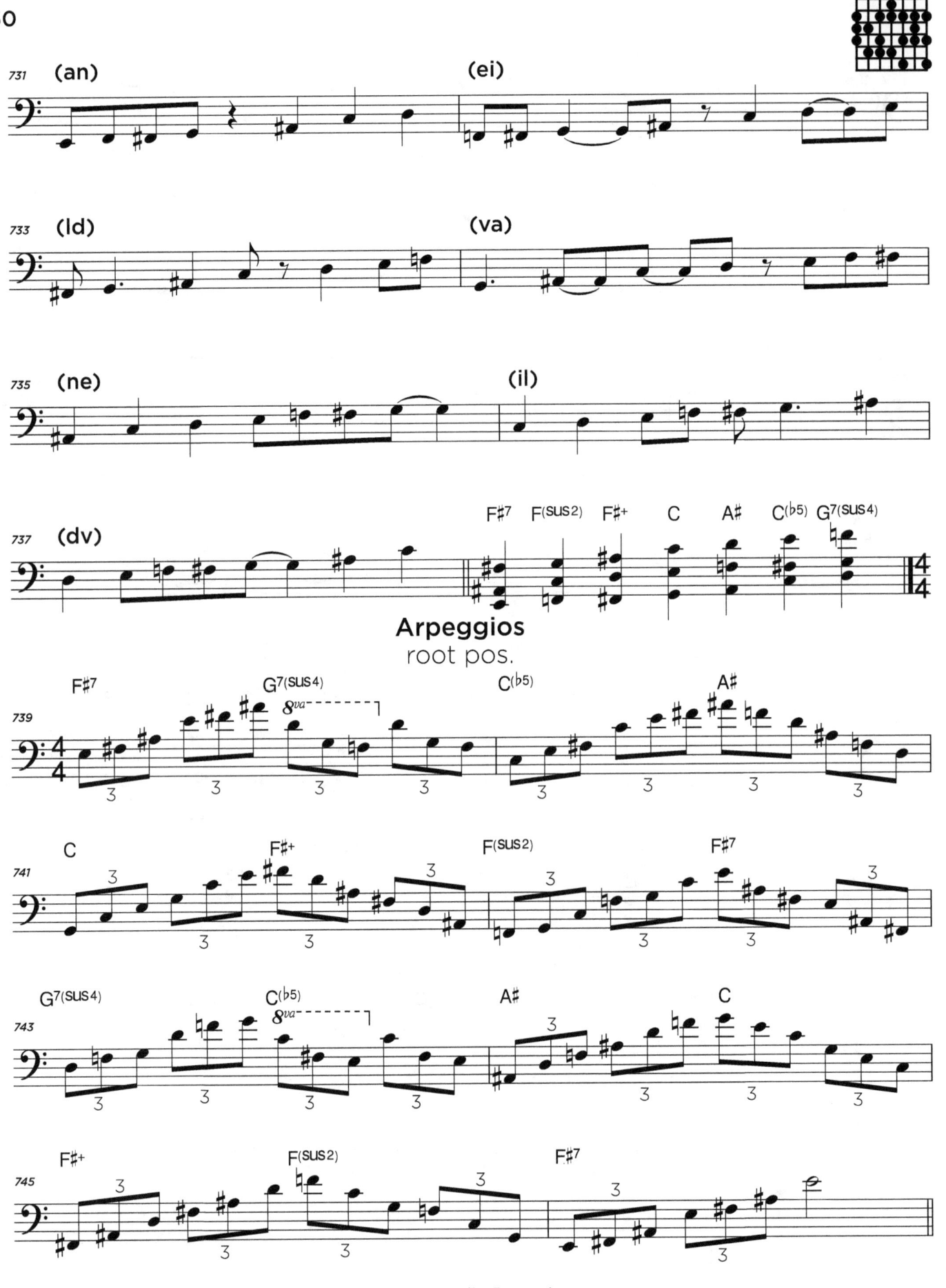

1st inv.

© 2017 by Felix Pastorius

763
Eb7
D(SUS2)
Eb+
A
765
G
A(b5)
E7(SUS4)
Eb7
767
D(SUS2)
Eb+
A
G
769
A(b5)
E7(SUS4)
Eb7
8va

2nd inv.

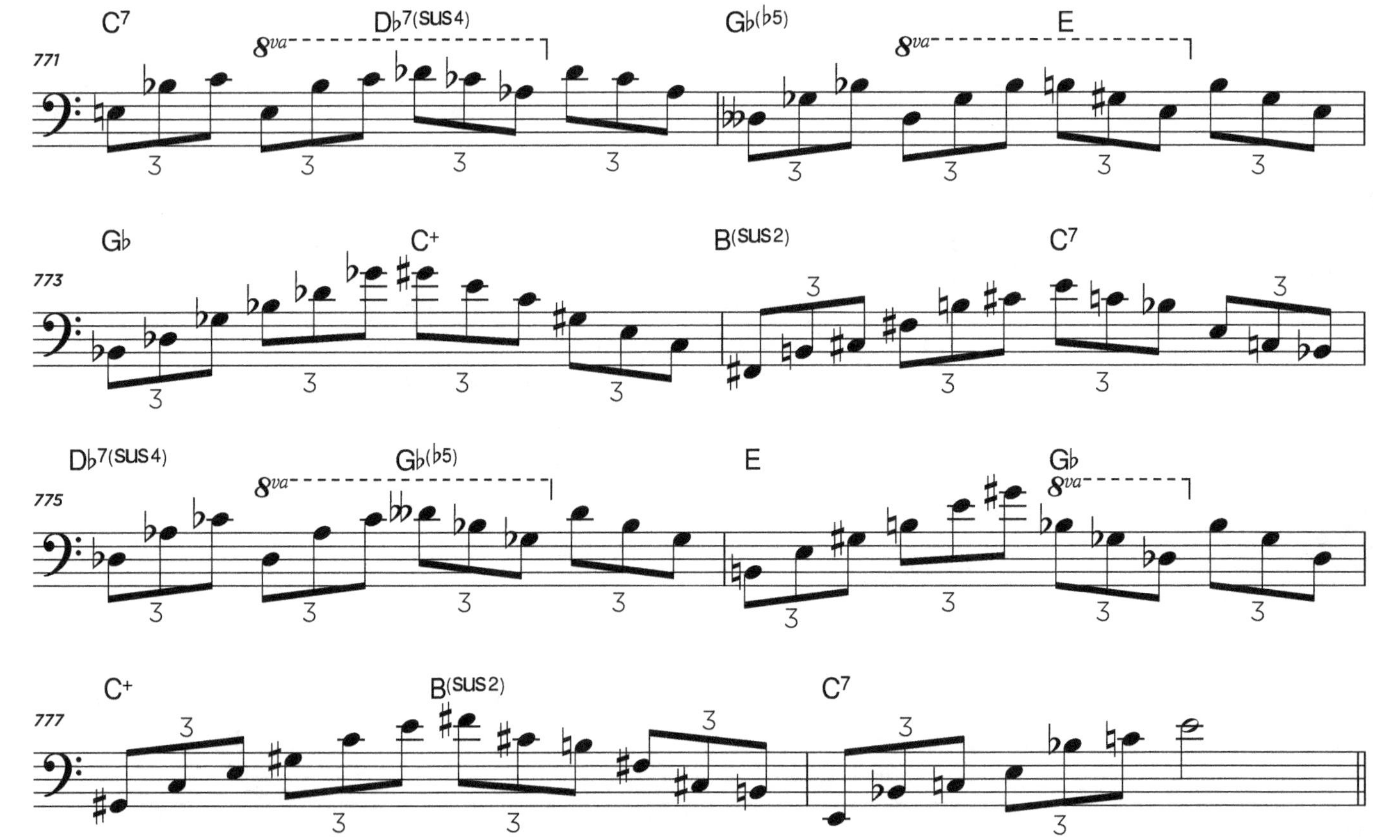
771
C7
Db7(SUS4)
Gb(b5)
E
773
Gb
C+
B(SUS2)
C7
775
Db7(SUS4)
Gb(b5)
E
Gb
777
C+
B(SUS2)
C7
8va

Voice Leading

#13

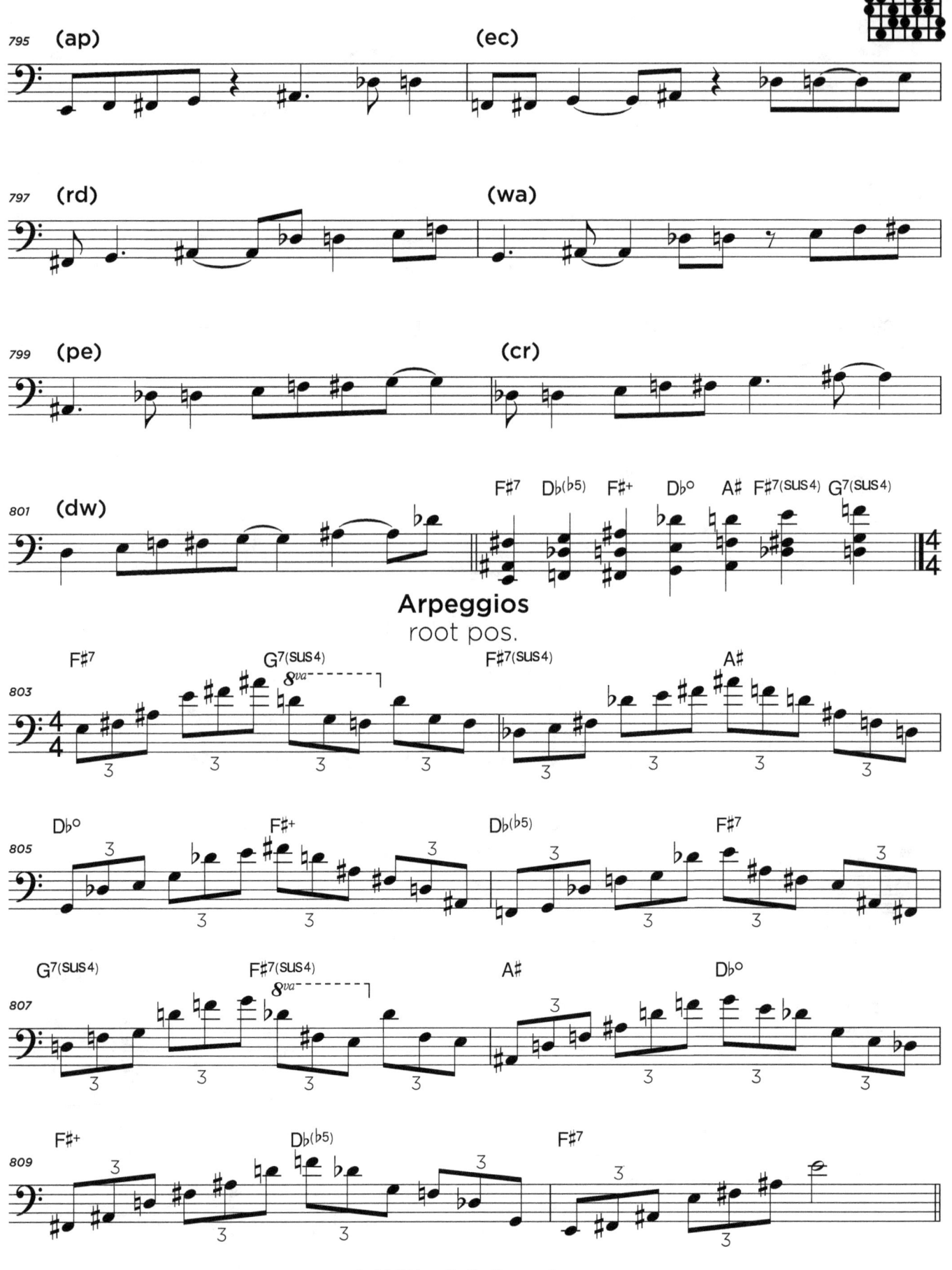

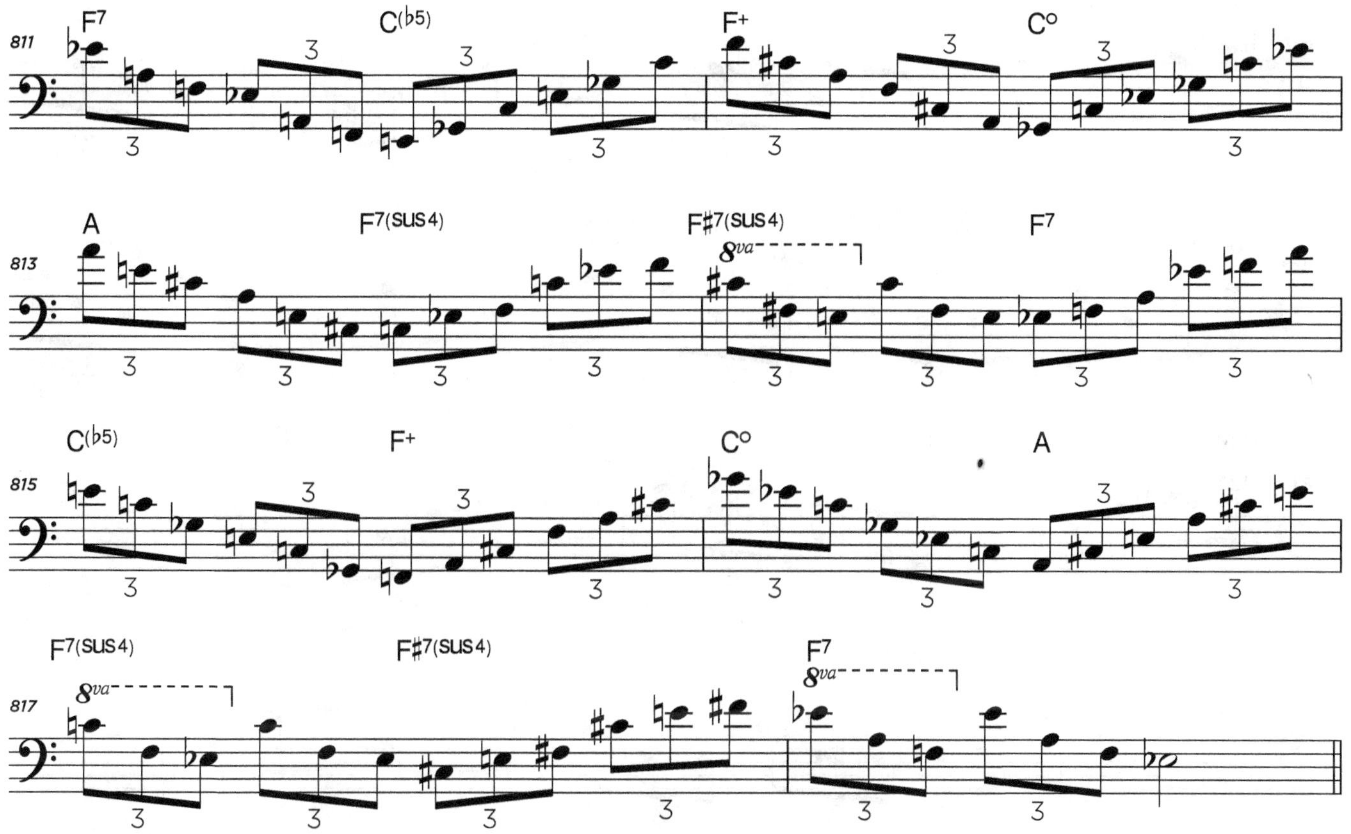
811
F7
C(♭5)
F+
C°
813
A
F7(SUS4)
F♯7(SUS4)
F7
815
C(♭5)
F+
C°
A
817
F7(SUS4)
F♯7(SUS4)
F7

1st inv.

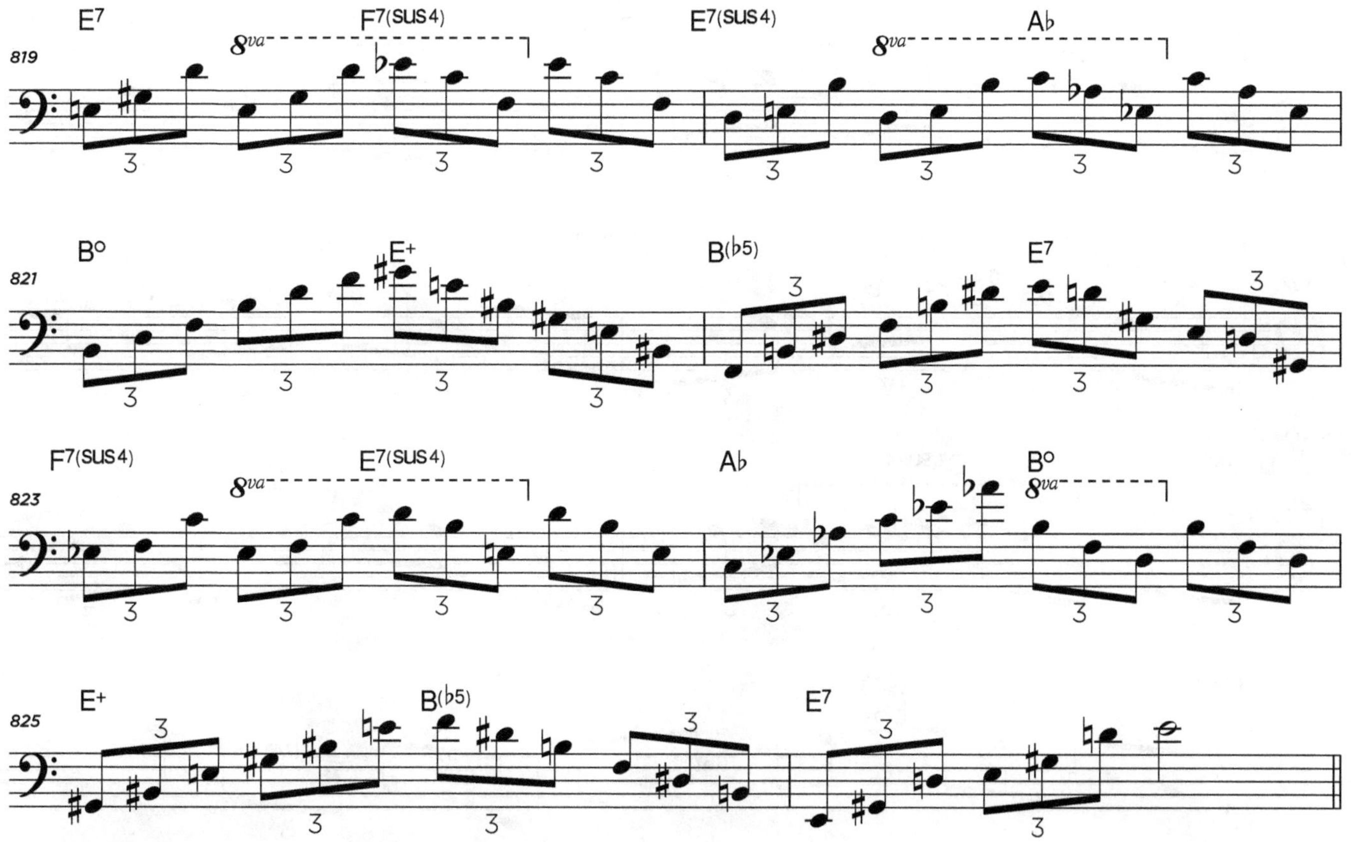
819
E7
F7(SUS4)
E7(SUS4)
A♭
821
B°
E+
B(♭5)
E7
823
F7(SUS4)
E7(SUS4)
A♭
B°
825
E+
B(♭5)
E7

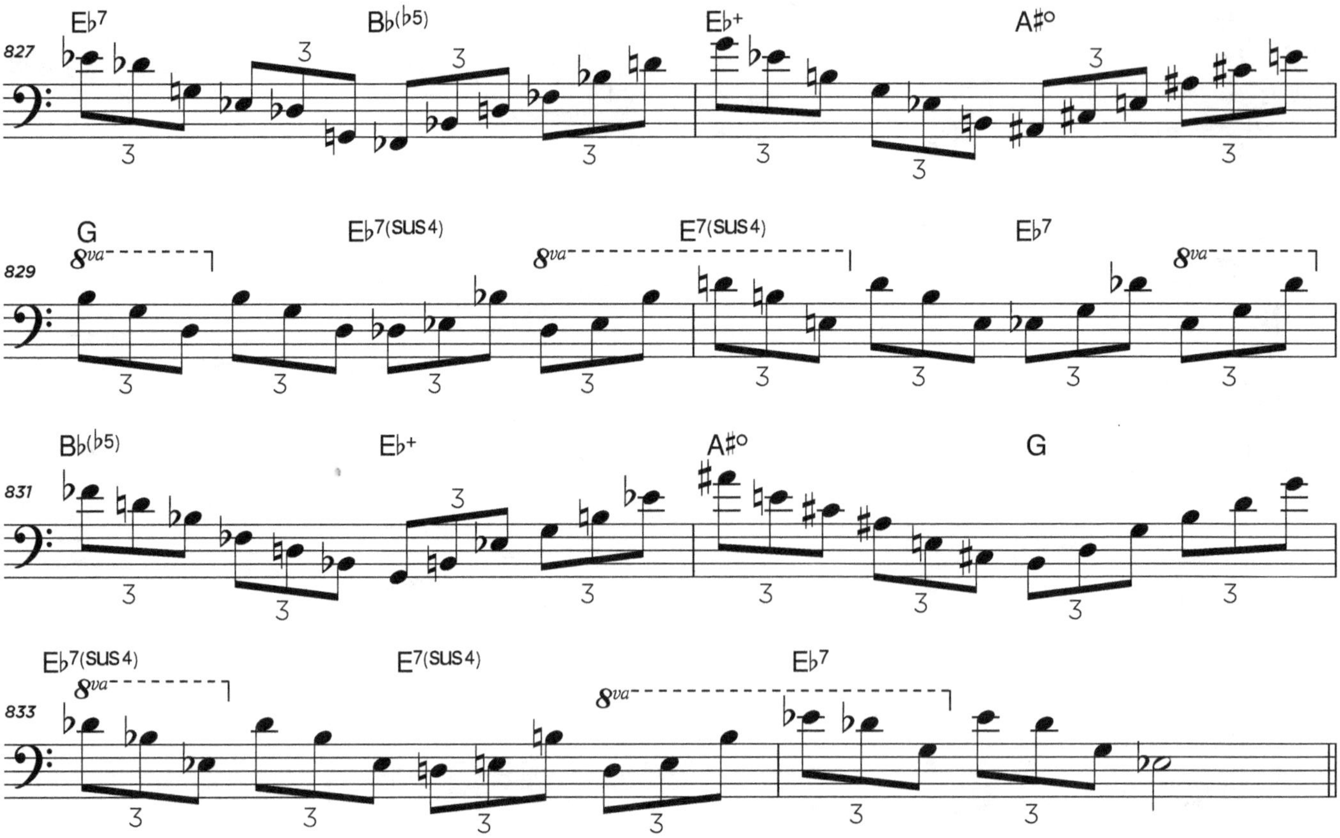
Eb7
Bb(b5)
Eb+
A#o
827
G
Eb7(SUS4)
E7(SUS4)
Eb7
829
Bb(b5)
Eb+
A#o
G
831
Eb7(SUS4)
E7(SUS4)
Eb7
833

2nd inv.

C7
Db7(SUS4)
C7(SUS4)
E
835
Go
C+
G(b5)
C7
837
Db7(SUS4)
C7(SUS4)
E
Go
839
C+
G(b5)
C7
841

Voice Leading

#14

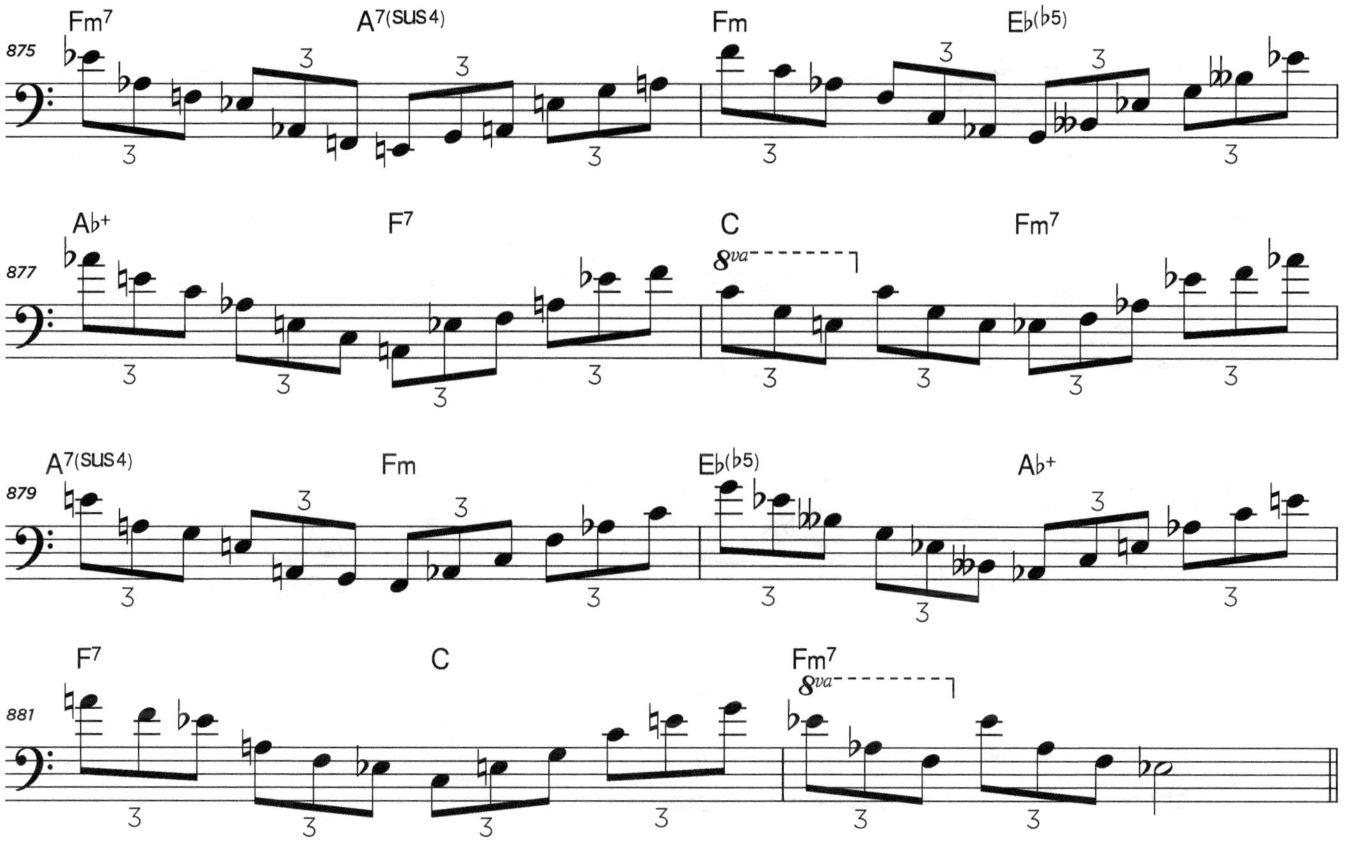
875
Fm7
A7(SUS4)
Fm
Eb(b5)
877
Ab+
F7
C
8va
Fm7
879
A7(SUS4)
Fm
Eb(b5)
Ab+
881
F7
C
Fm7
8va

1st inv.

883
Em7
8va
B
E7
G+
8va
885
D(b5)
Em
Ab7(SUS4)
Em7
887
B
8va
E7
G+
D(b5)
889
Em
Ab7(SUS4)
Em7

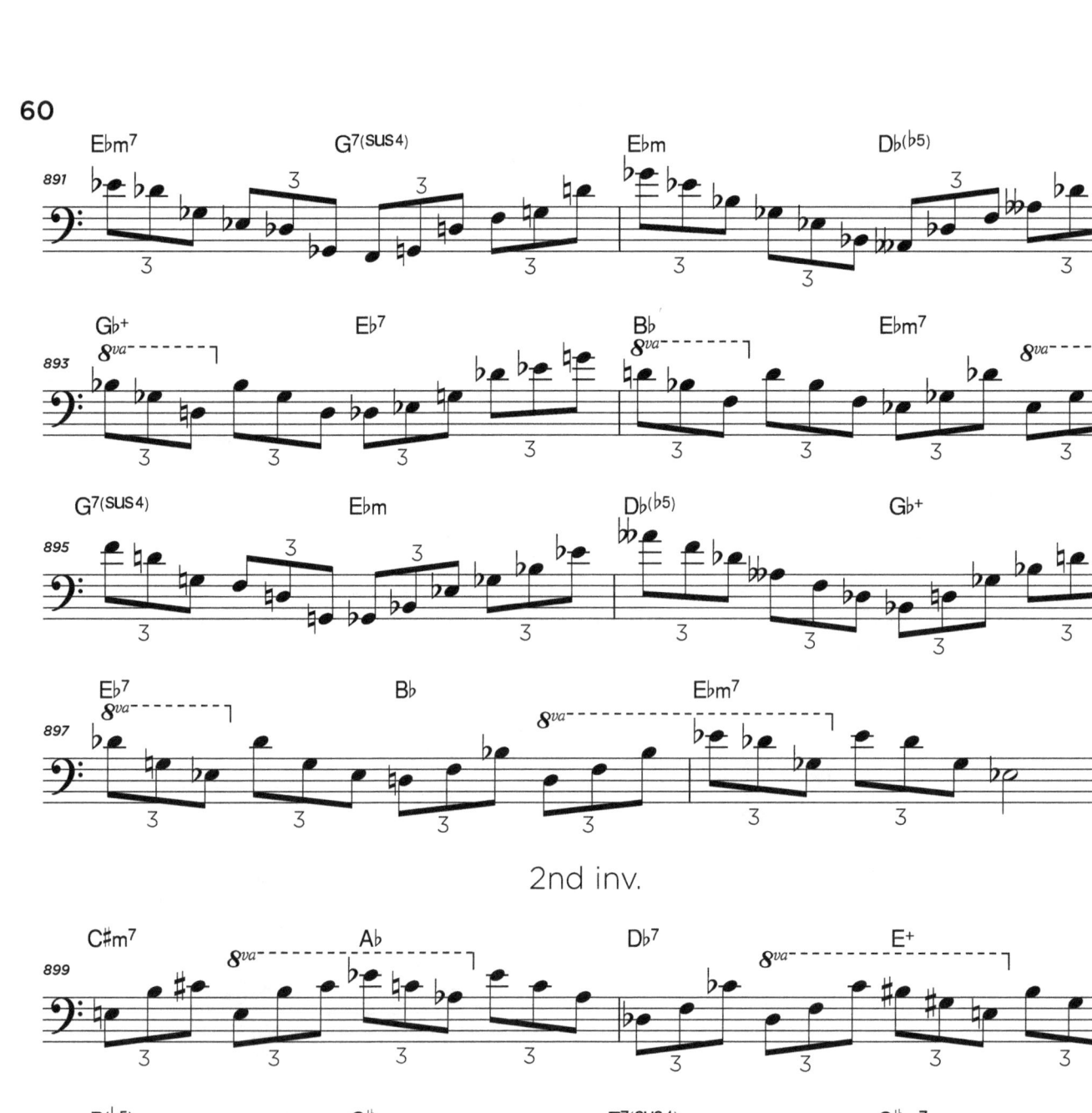

2nd inv.

© 2017 by Felix Pastorius

Voice Leading

#15

939
Fm7
E°
Fm
E♭
941
A♭+
B♭(SUS 4)
C
8va
Fm7
943
E°
Fm
E♭
A♭+
945
B♭(SUS 4)
8va
C
Fm7
8va

1st inv.

947
Em7
8va
B
A(SUS 4)
G+
8va
949
D
Em
D♯°
Em7
951
B
8va
A(SUS 4)
G+
D
953
Em
D♯°
Em7

955
Ebm7
Do
Ebm
Db
957
Gb+
Ab(sus4)
Bb
Ebm7
8va
959
Do
Ebm
Db
Gb+
961
Ab(sus4)
Bb
Ebm7
8va

2nd inv.

963
C#m7
Ab
F#(sus4)
E+
8va
965
B
C#m
Co
C#m7
967
Ab
F#(sus4)
E+
B
8va
969
C#m
Co
C#m7

Voice Leading

#16

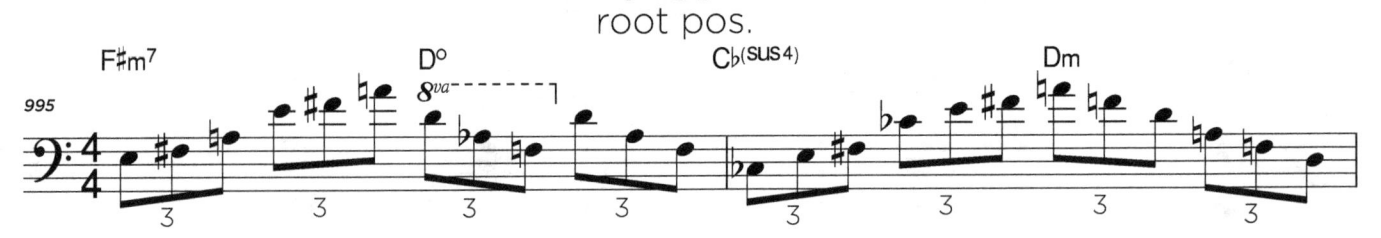

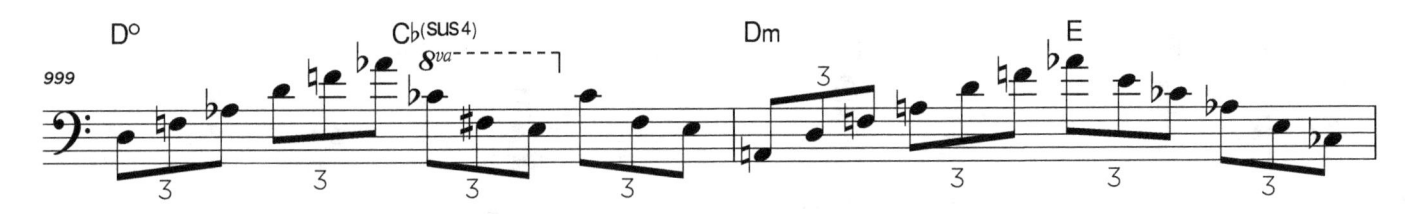

1003
Fm7
E°
D♭
E♭
1005
C♯m
B♭(SUS4)
C♯°
Fm7
1007
E°
D♭
E♭
C♯m
1009
B♭(SUS4)
C♯°
Fm7
8va

1st inv.

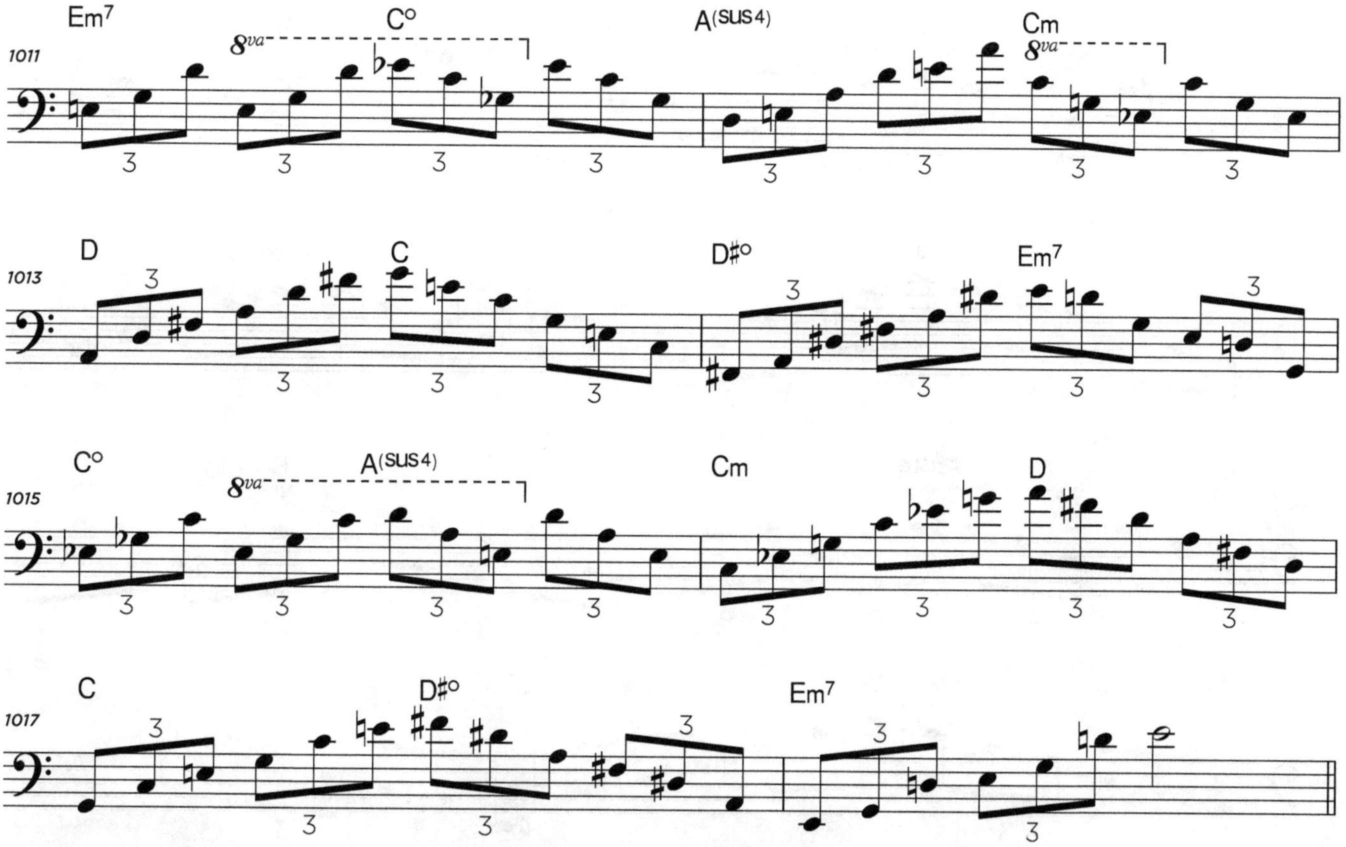
1011
Em7
C°
A(SUS4)
Cm
1013
D
C
D♯°
Em7
1015
C°
A(SUS4)
Cm
D
1017
C
D♯°
Em7
8va

1019
Ebm7
Do
B
Db
1021
Bm
Ab(sus4)
Bo
Ebm7
1023
Do
B
Db
Bm
1025
Ab(sus4)
Bo
Ebm7

2nd inv.

1027
C#m7
Ao
F#(sus4)
Am
1029
B
A
Co
C#m7
1031
Ao
F#(sus4)
Am
B
1033
A
Co
C#m7

Voice Leading

#17

1051 (bu)
(cg)
1053 (mj)
(gb)
1055 (uc)
(gm)
1057 (jg)
F♯m7 Fm F♯m A♭+ A+ C(♭5) C♯
Arpeggios
root pos.
1059 F♯m7 C♯ 8va C(♭5) A+
1061 A♭+ F♯m Fm F♯m7
1063 C♯ C(♭5) 8va A+ A♭+
1065 F♯m Fm F♯m7

Fm7
Em
Fm
G+
1067
Ab+
B(b5)
C
Fm7
1069
8va
Em
Fm
G+
Ab+
1071
B(b5)
C
Fm7
1073
8va
8va

1st inv.

Em7
B
Bb(b5)
G+
1075
8va
8va
Gb+
Em
Ebm
Em7
1077
B
Bb(b5)
G+
Gb+
1079
8va
8va
Em
Ebm
Em7
1081

Ebm7 Dm Ebm F+
1083
Gb+ A(b5) Bb Ebm7
1085
8va
Dm Ebm F+ Gb+
1087
A(b5) Bb Ebm7
1089
8va

2nd inv.

C#m7 Ab G(b5) E+
1091
8va
Eb+ C#m Cm C#m7
1093
Ab G(b5) E+ Eb+
1095
8va
C#m Cm C#m7
1097

Voice Leading

#18

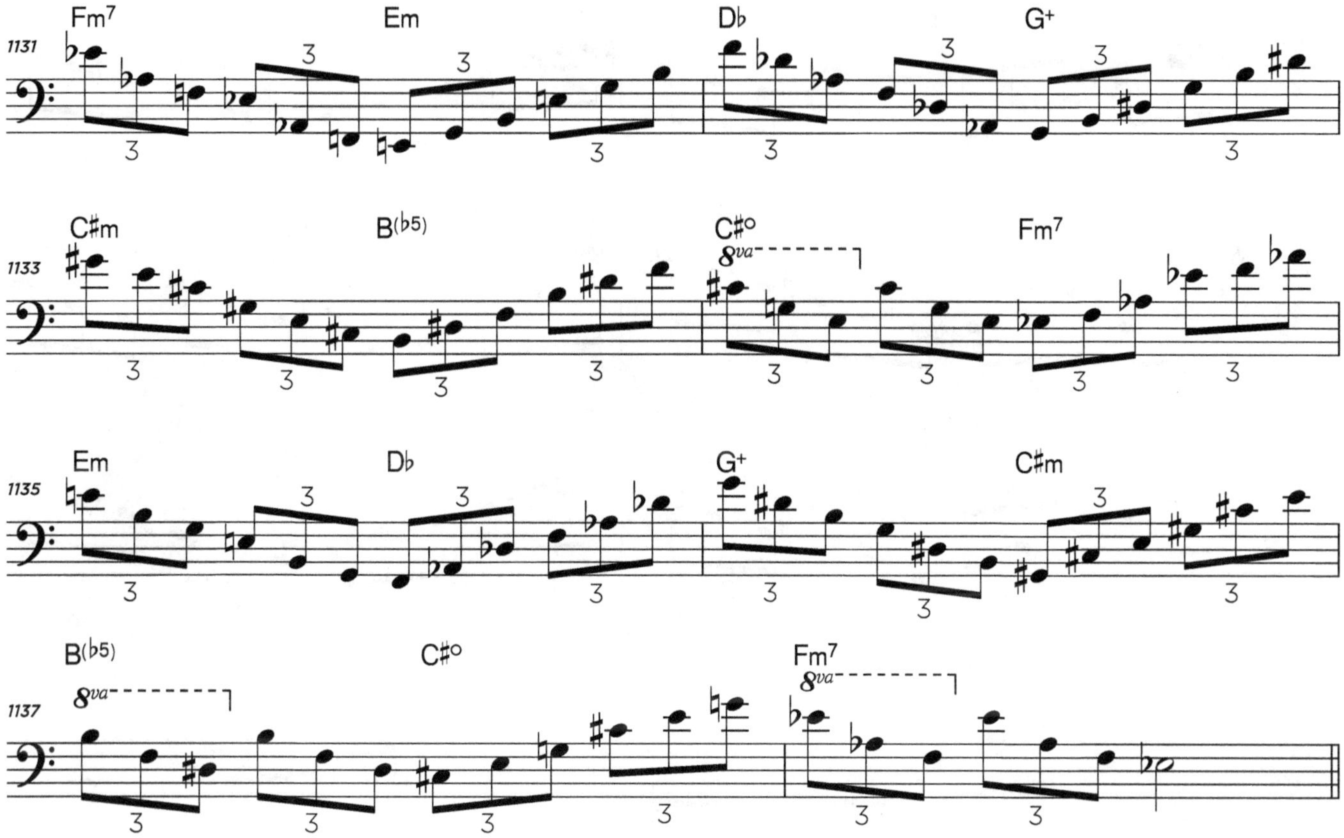
1131
Fm7 Em Db G+
1133
C♯m B(♭5) C♯o 8va Fm7
1135
Em Db G+ C♯m
1137
B(♭5) 8va C♯o Fm7 8va

1st inv.

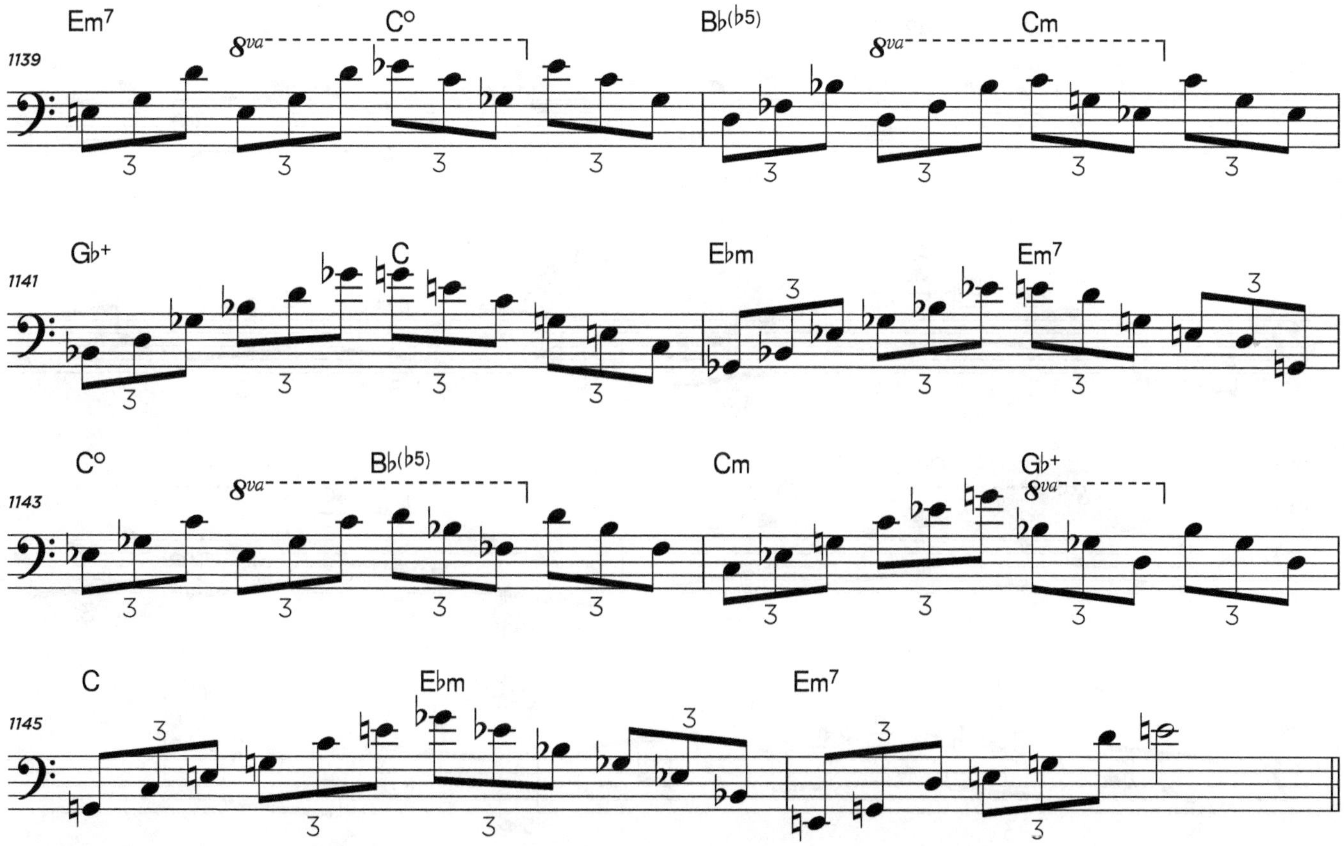
1139
Em7 8va Co B♭(♭5) 8va Cm
1141
G♭+ C E♭m Em7
1143
Co 8va B♭(♭5) Cm G♭+ 8va
1145
C E♭m Em7

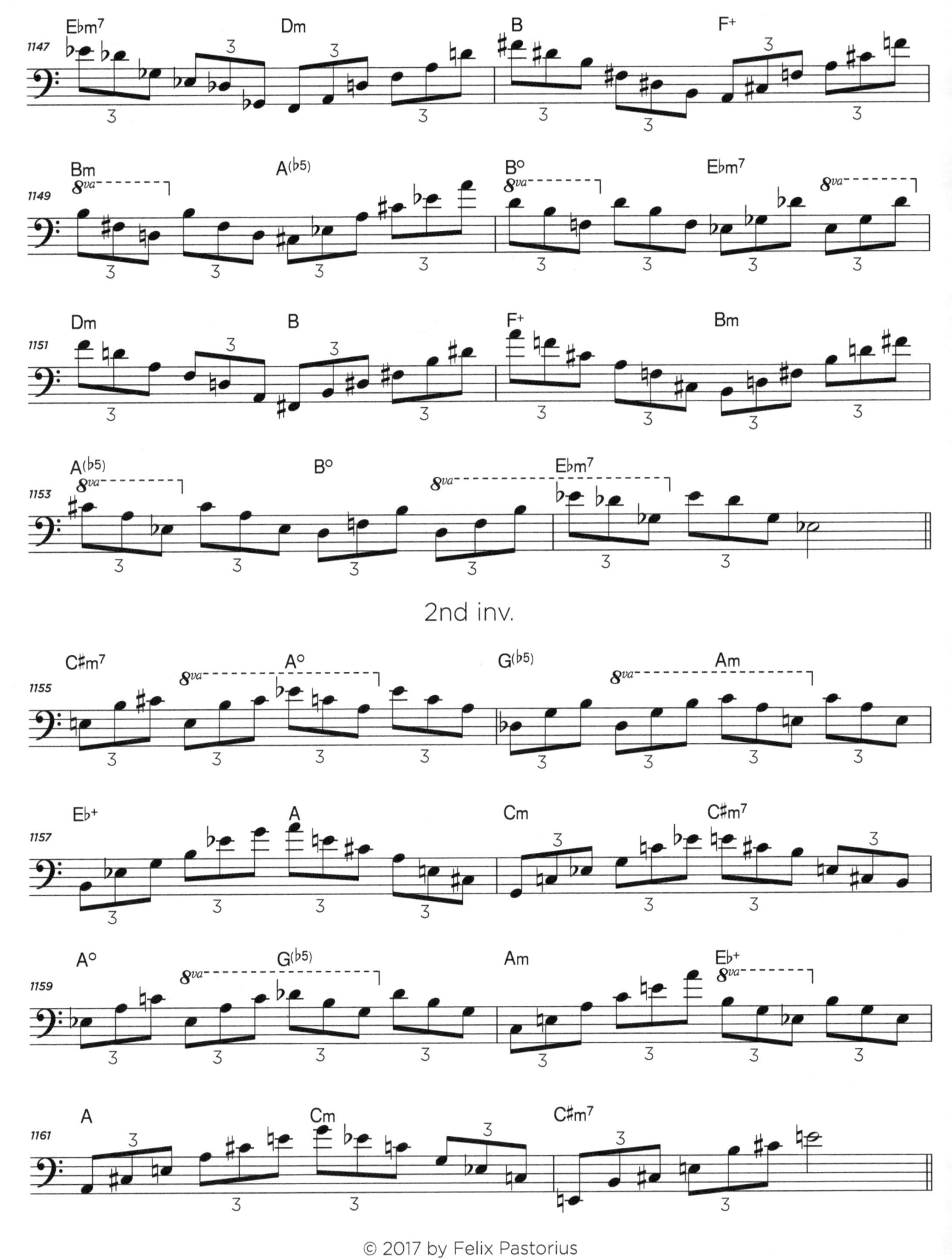

© 2017 by Felix Pastorius

Voice Leading

#19

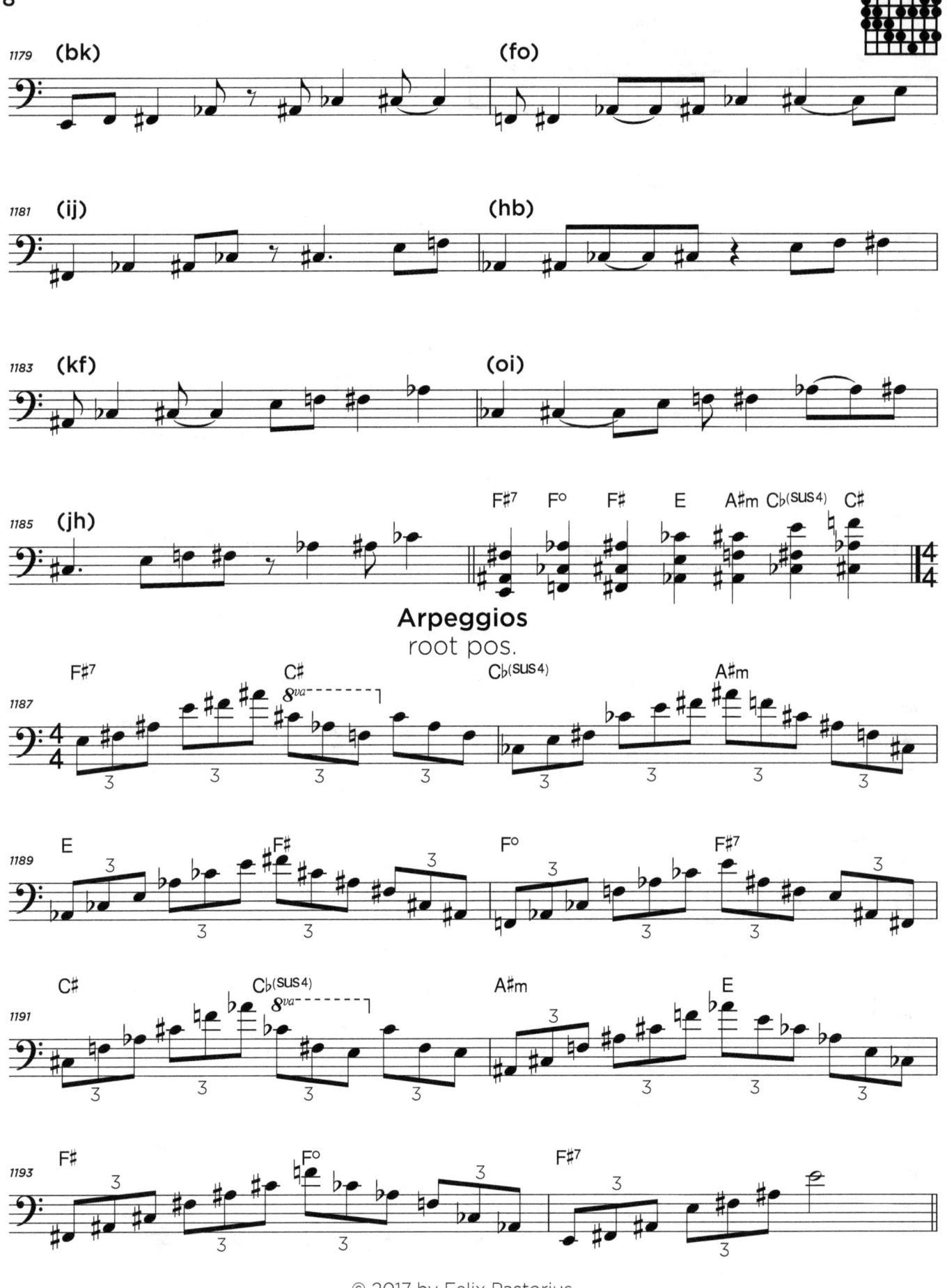

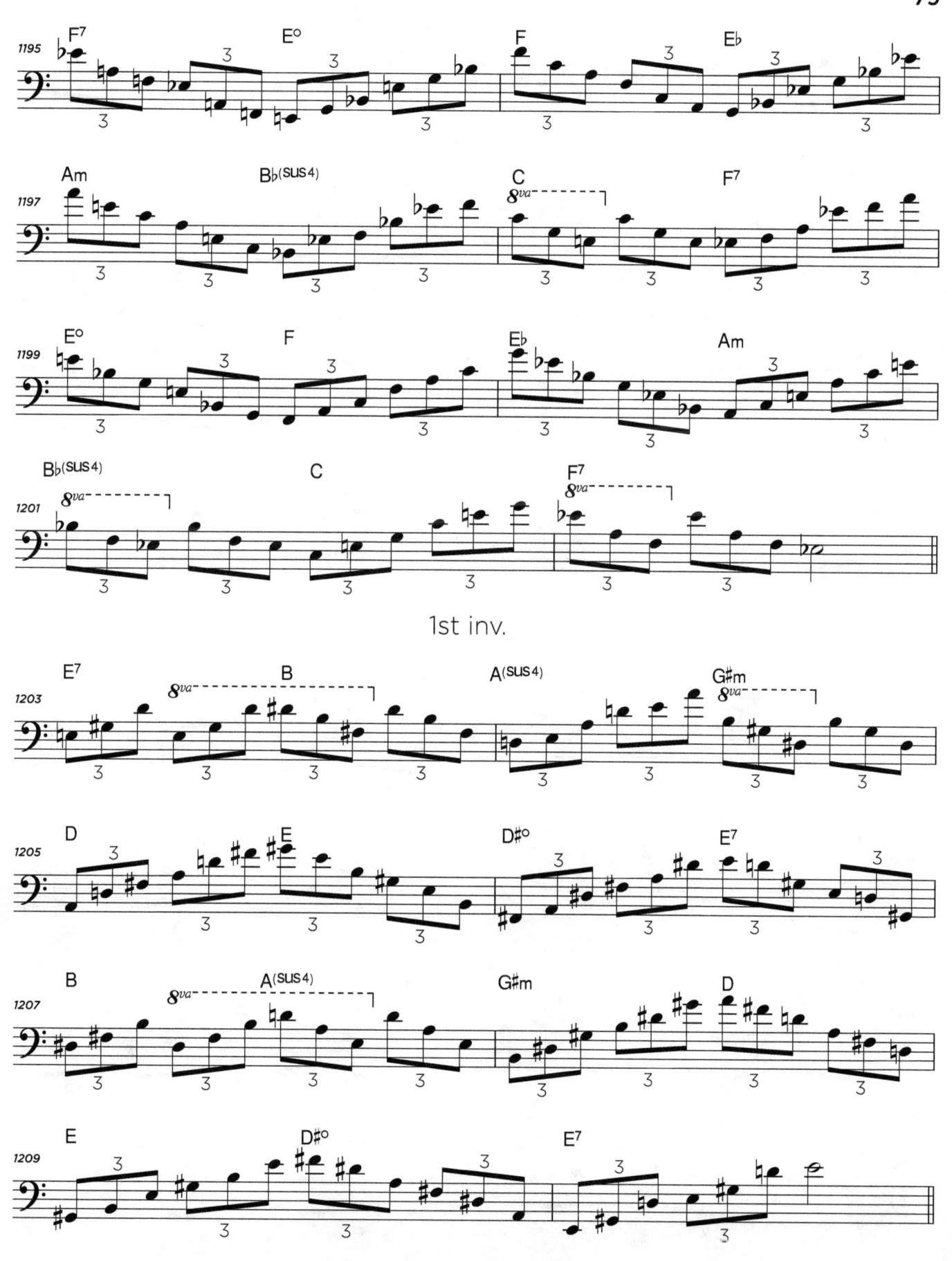

© 2017 by Felix Pastorius

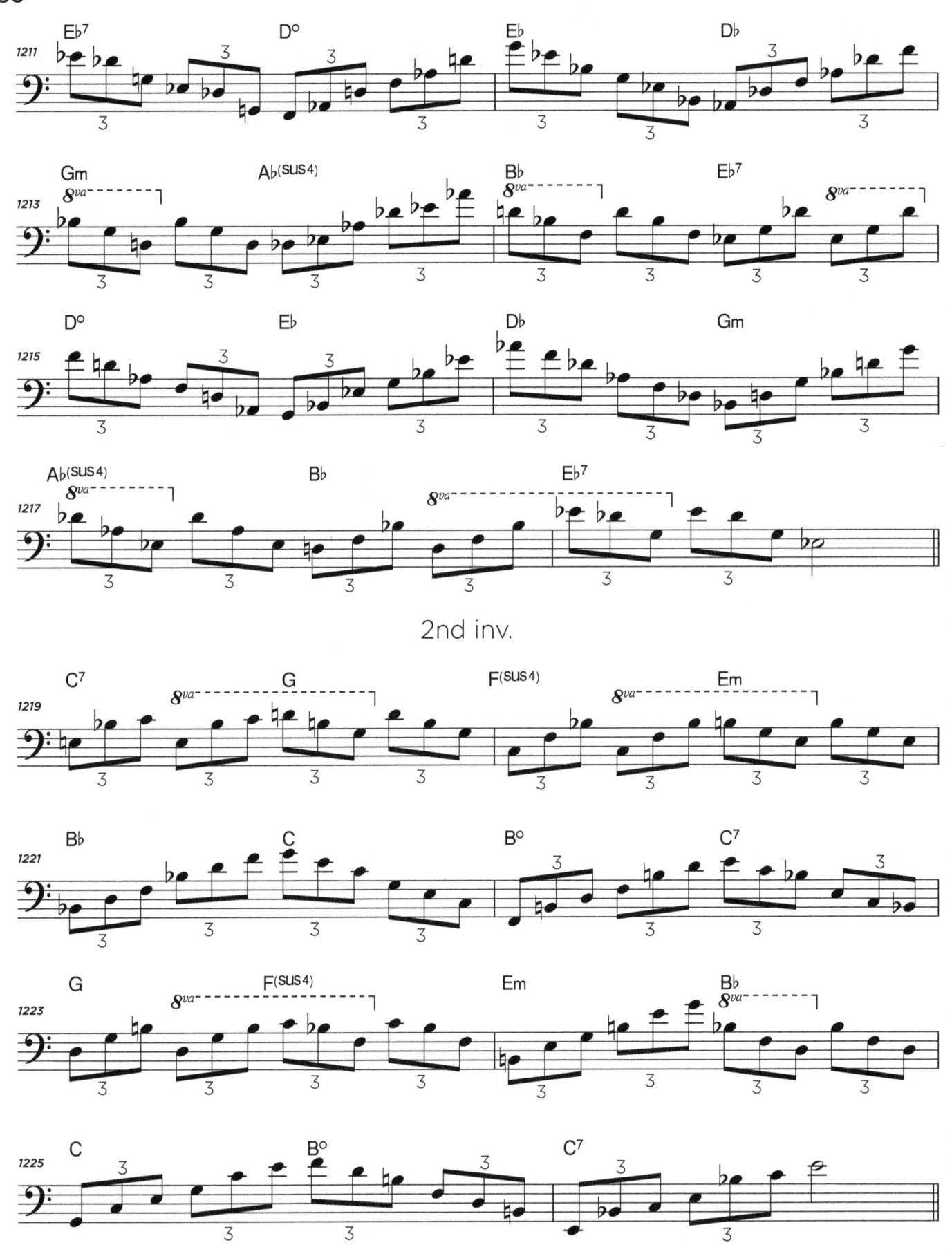

2nd inv.

© 2017 by Felix Pastorius

Voice Leading

#20

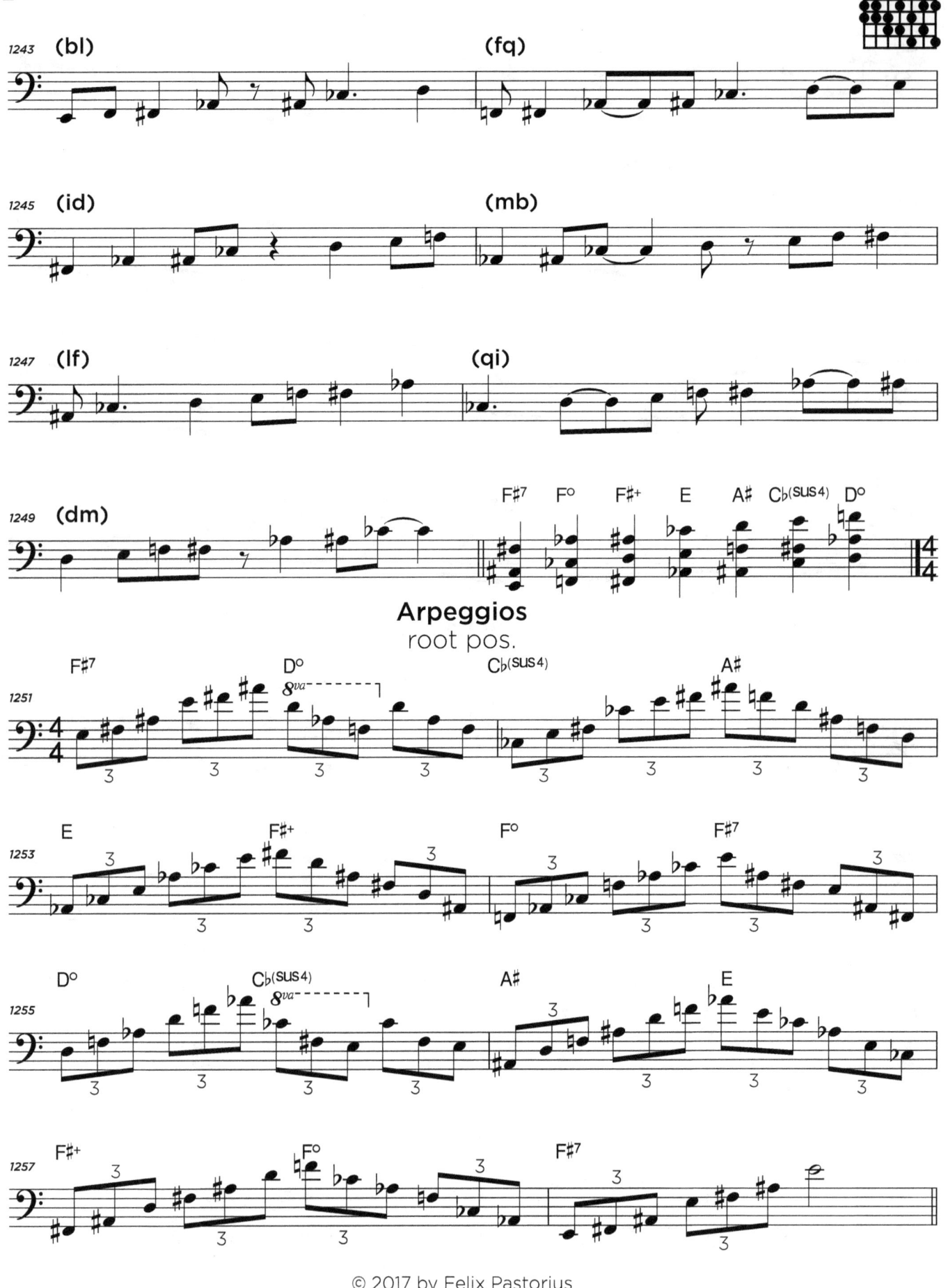

1259
F7
E°
F+
E♭
1261
A
B♭(SUS4)
C♯°
F7
1263
E°
F+
E♭
A
1265
B♭(SUS4)
C♯°
F7

1st inv.

1267
E7
C°
A(SUS4)
A♭
1269
D
E+
D♯°
E7
1271
C°
A(SUS4)
A♭
D
1273
E+
D♯°
E7

1275
E♭7
D°
E♭+
D♭
1277
G
A♭(SUS4)
B°
E♭7
1279
D°
E♭+
D♭
G
1281
A♭(SUS4)
B°
E♭7

2nd inv.

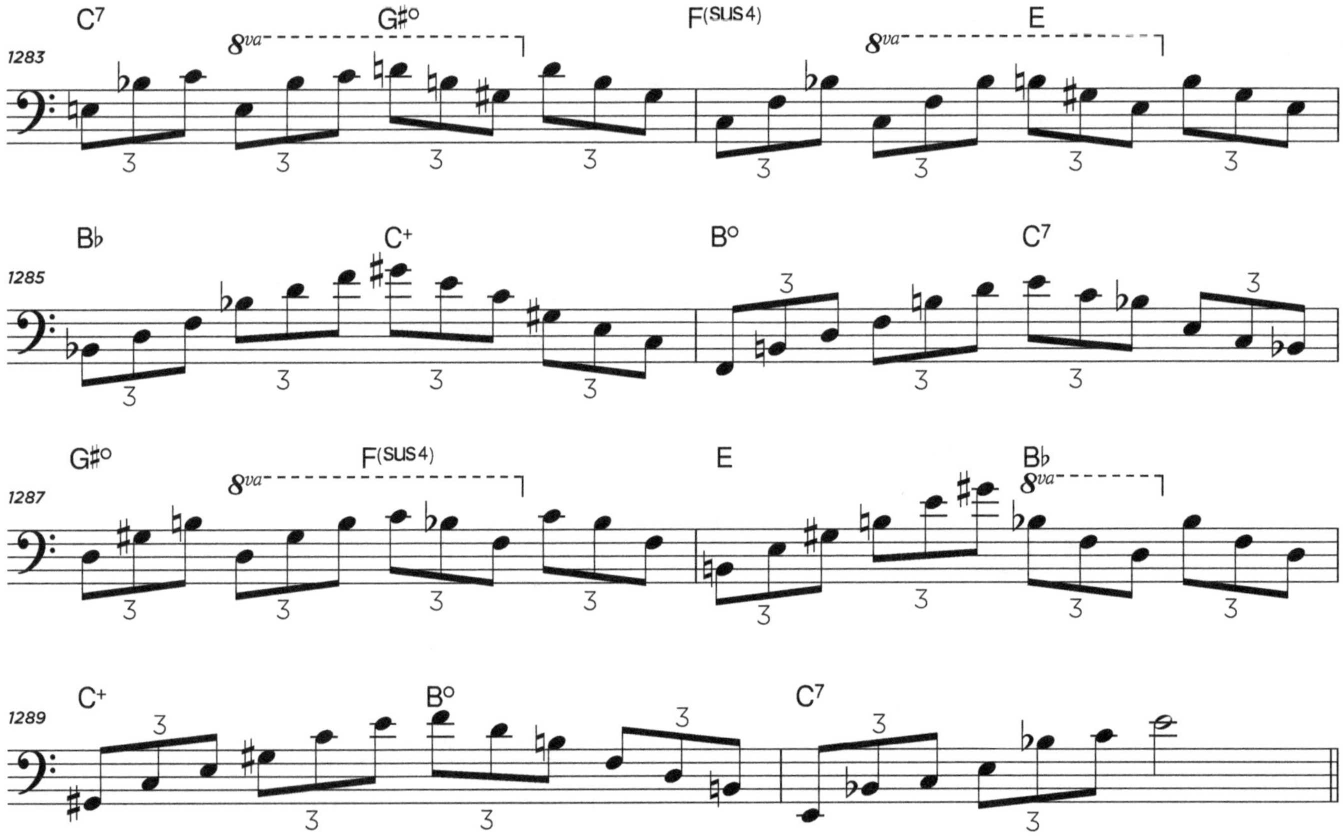
1283
C7
G♯°
F(SUS4)
E
1285
B♭
C+
B°
C7
1287
G♯°
F(SUS4)
E
B♭
1289
C+
B°
C7

Voice Leading

#21

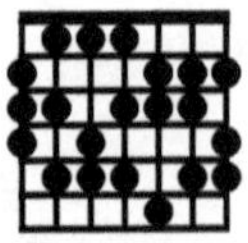

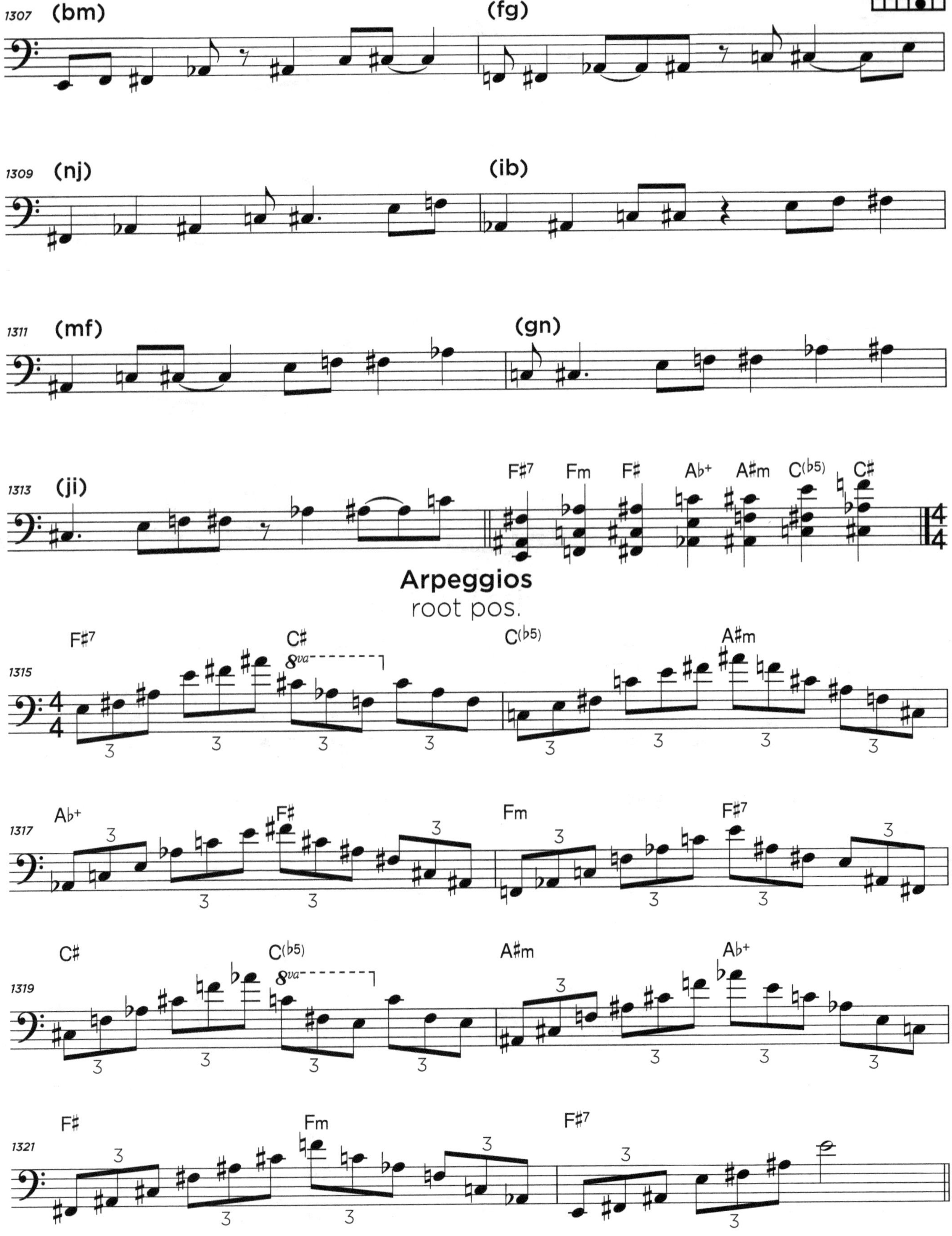
1307
(bm)
(fg)
1309
(nj)
(ib)
1311
(mf)
(gn)
1313
(ji)
F♯7 Fm F♯ A♭+ A♯m C(♭5) C♯
Arpeggios
root pos.
1315
F♯7 C♯ C(♭5) A♯m
8va
1317
A♭+ F♯ Fm F♯7
1319
C♯ C(♭5) A♯m A♭+
8va
1321
F♯ Fm F♯7

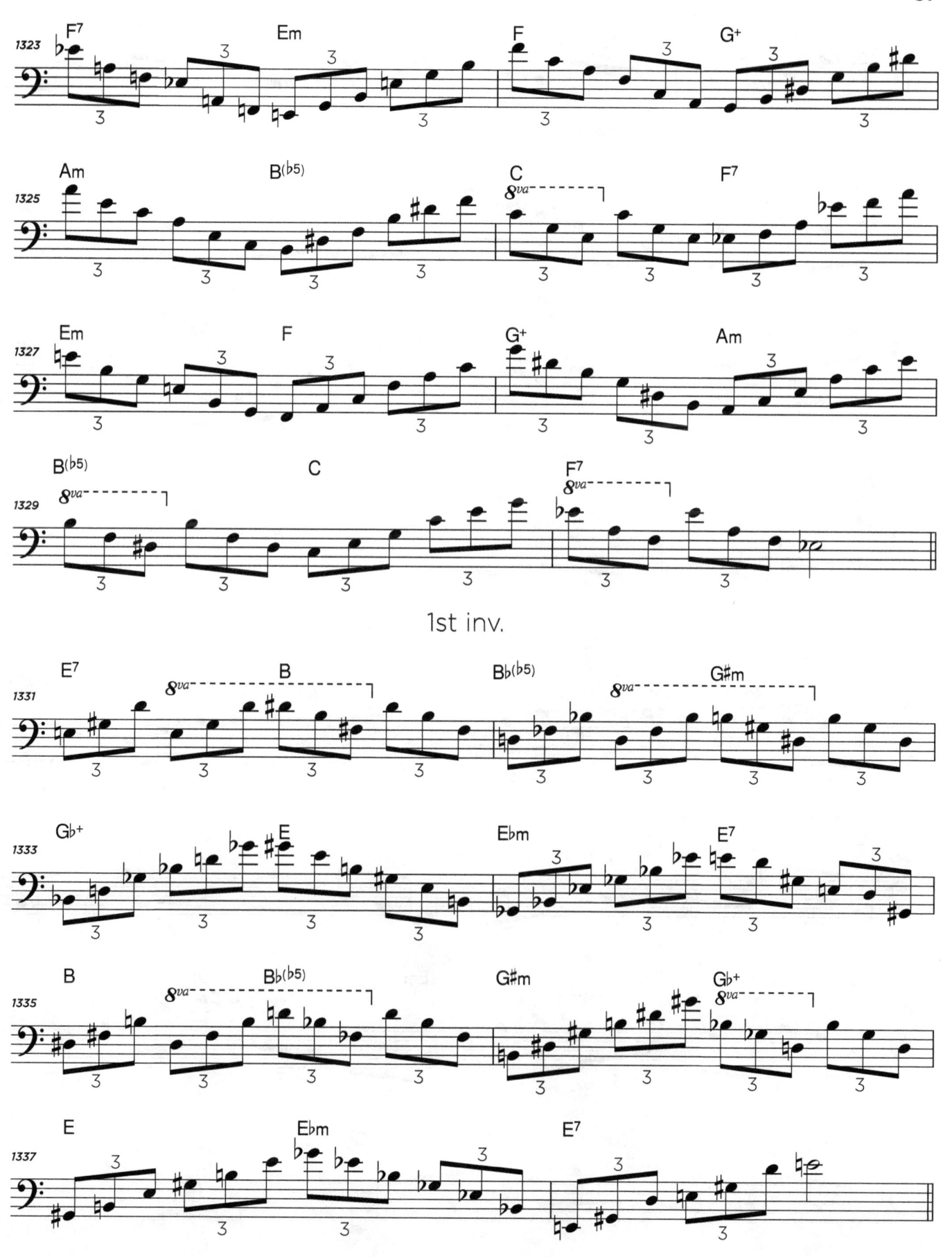

87

© 2017 by Felix Pastorius

© 2017 by Felix Pastorius

Voice Leading

#22

91

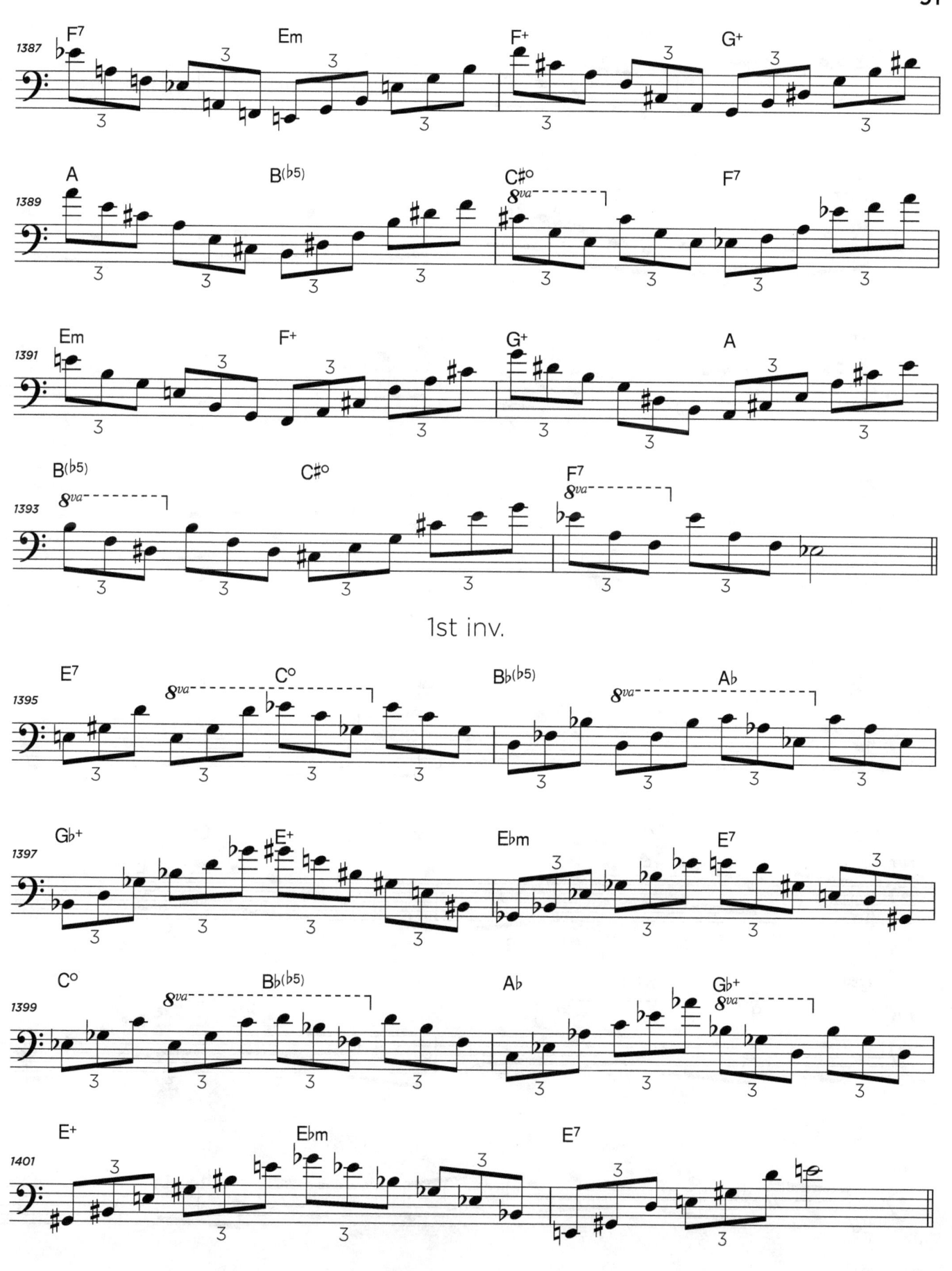

Eb7
Dm
Eb+
F+
1403
G
A(b5)
Bo
Eb7
1405
8va
Dm
Eb+
F+
G
1407
A(b5)
Bo
Eb7
1409
8va

2nd inv.

C7
G#o
Gb(b5)
E
1411
8va
D+
C+
Bm
C7
1413
G#o
Gb(b5)
E
D+
1415
8va
C+
Bm
C7
1417

Voice Leading

#23

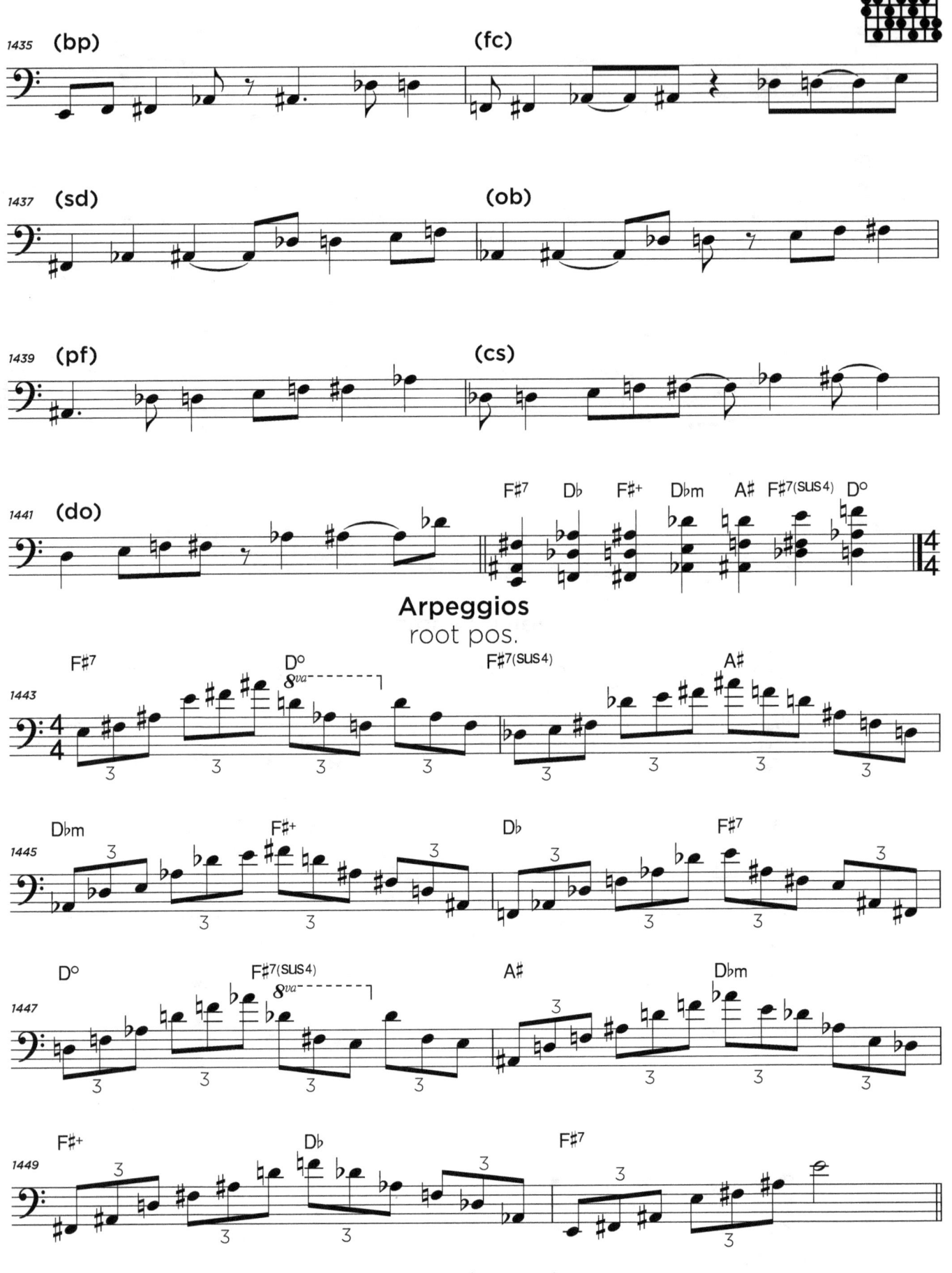

1451
F7
C
F+
Cm
1453
A
F7(SUS 4)
C♯o
F7
1455
C
F+
Cm
A
1457
F7(SUS 4)
C♯o
F7
8va

1st inv.

1459
E7
Co
E7(SUS 4)
A♭
1461
Bm
E+
B
E7
1463
Co
E7(SUS 4)
A♭
Bm
1465
E+
B
E7
8va

1467
E♭7
B♭
E♭+
B♭m
1469
G
E♭7(SUS4)
B°
E♭7
1471
B♭
E♭+
B♭m
G
1473
E♭7(SUS4)
B°
E♭7

2nd inv.

1475
C7
G♯°
C7(SUS4)
E
1477
Gm
C+
G
C7
1479
G♯°
C7(SUS4)
E
Gm
1481
C+
G
C7

Voice Leading

#24

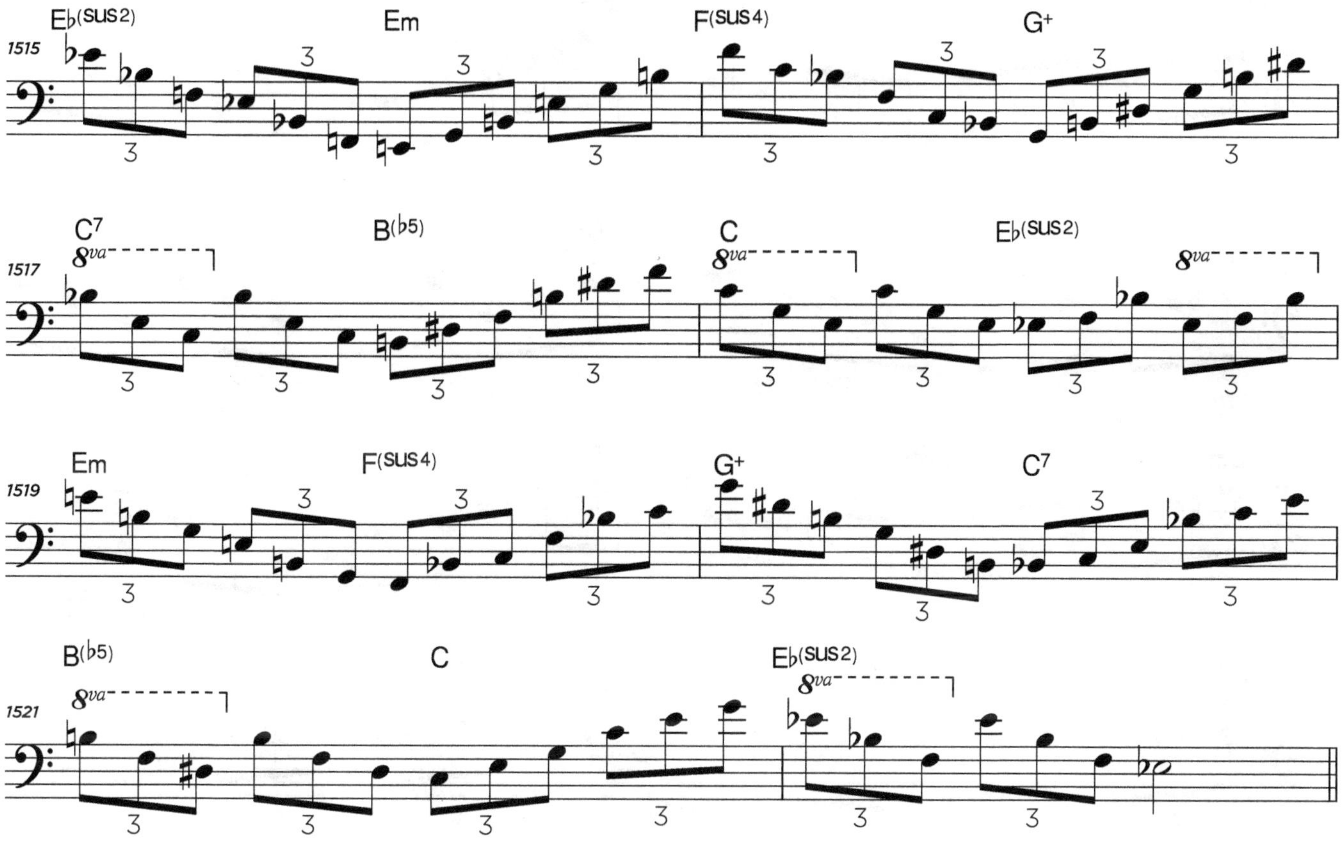
1515
E♭(sus2) Em F(sus4) G+
1517
C7 B(♭5) C E♭(sus2)
1519
Em F(sus4) G+ C7
1521
B(♭5) C E♭(sus2)
8va

1st inv.

1523
D(sus2) B B♭(♭5) B7
1525
G♭+ E(sus4) E♭m D(sus2)
1527
B B♭(♭5) B7 G♭+
1529
E(sus4) E♭m D(sus2)
8va

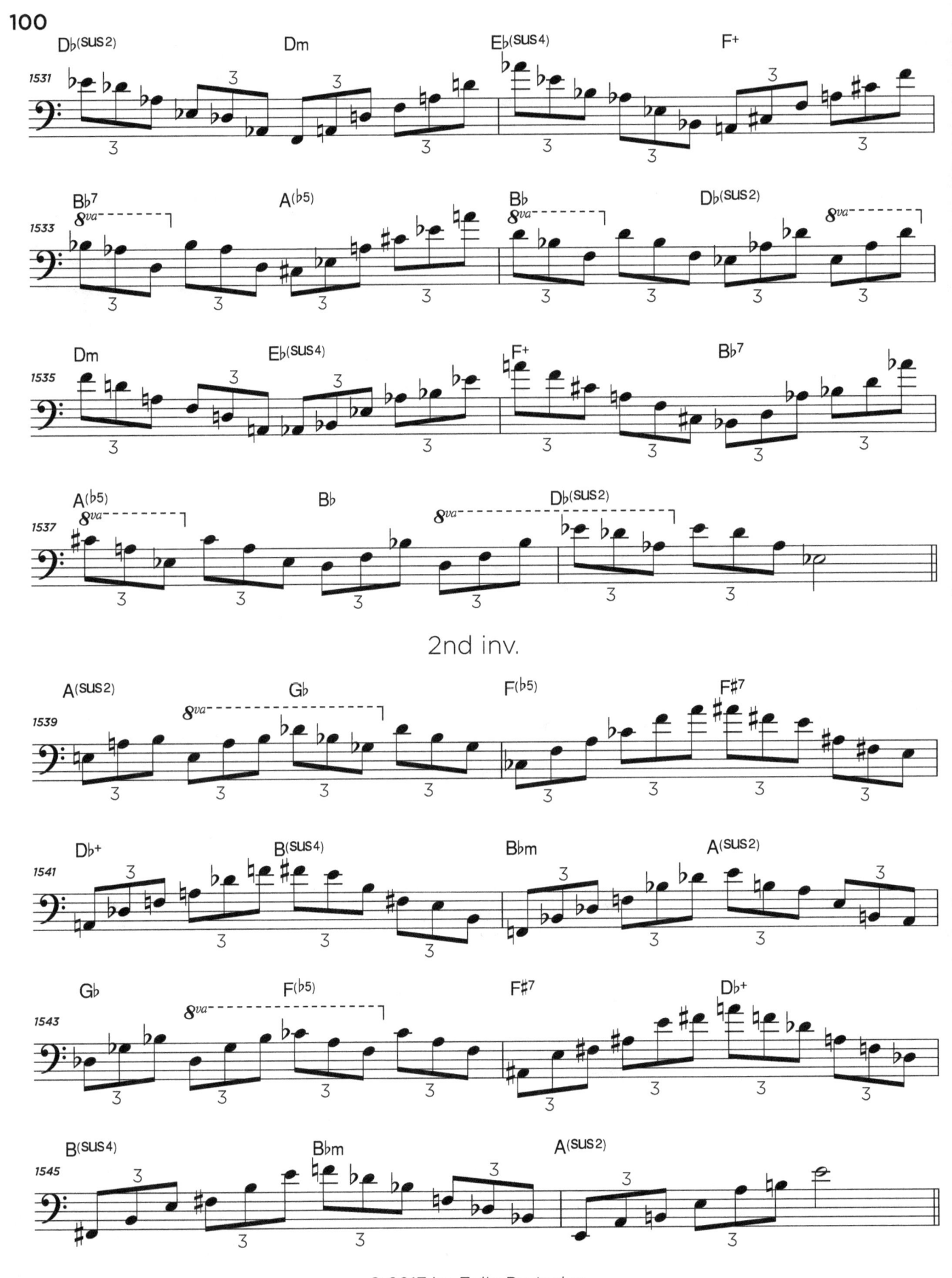

© 2017 by Felix Pastorius

Voice Leading

#25

1563 (bf)
(ki)
1565 (od)
(pb)
1567 (fk)
(io)
1569 (dp)
E(sus2) Fm Bm Ab+ Bo C(b5) Do
Arpeggios
root pos.
1571 E(sus2) Do C(b5) Bo
1573 Ab+ Bm Fm E(sus2)
1575 Do C(b5) Bo Ab+
1577 Bm Fm E(sus2)

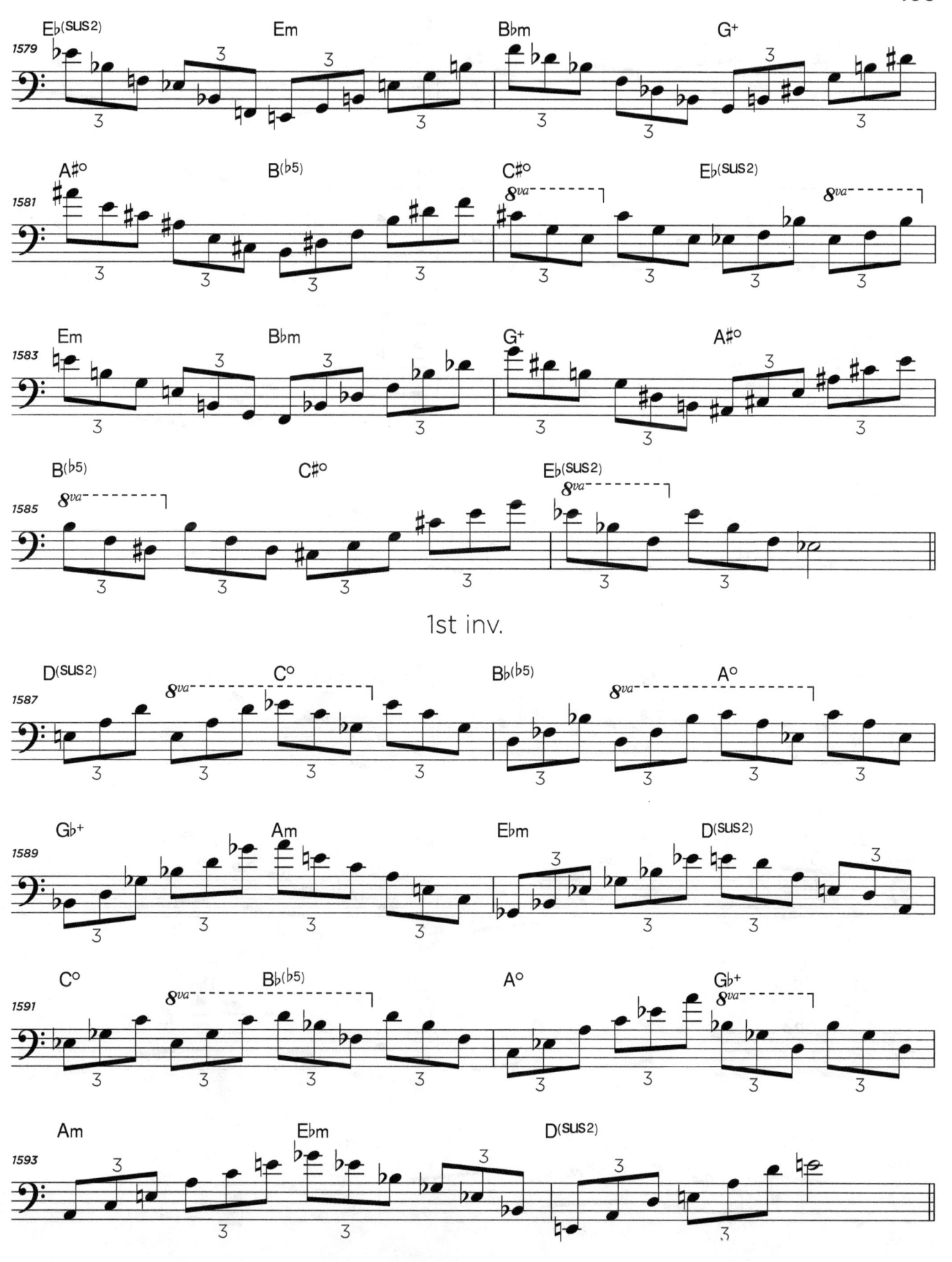

© 2017 by Felix Pastorius

1595
D♭(SUS2)
Dm
G♯m
F+
1597
G♯o
A(♭5)
Bo
D♭(SUS2)
1599
Dm
G♯m
F+
G♯o
1601
A(♭5)
Bo
D♭(SUS2)

2nd inv.

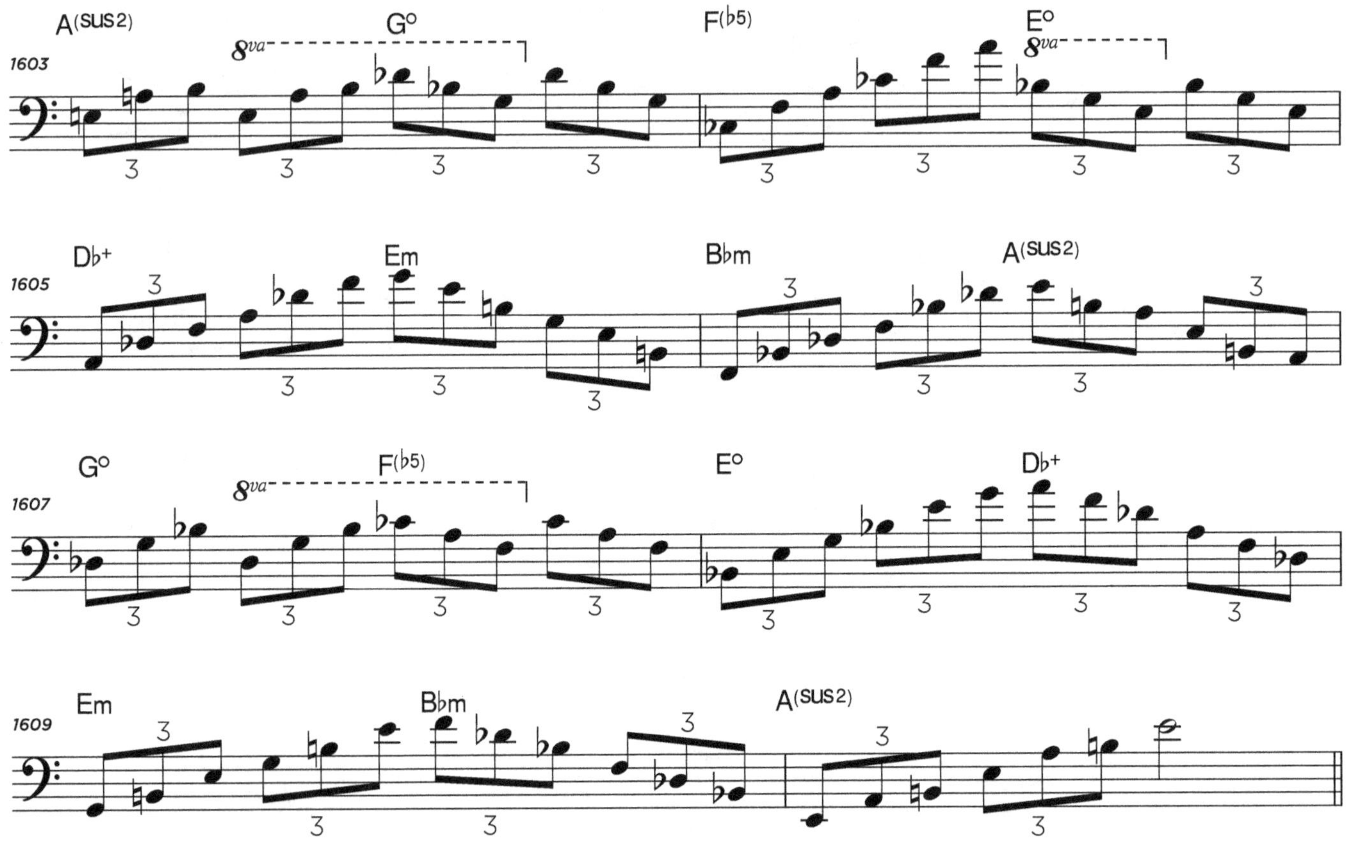
1603
A(SUS2)
Go
F(♭5)
Eo
1605
D♭+
Em
B♭m
A(SUS2)
1607
Go
F(♭5)
Eo
D♭+
1609
Em
B♭m
A(SUS2)

Voice Leading

#26

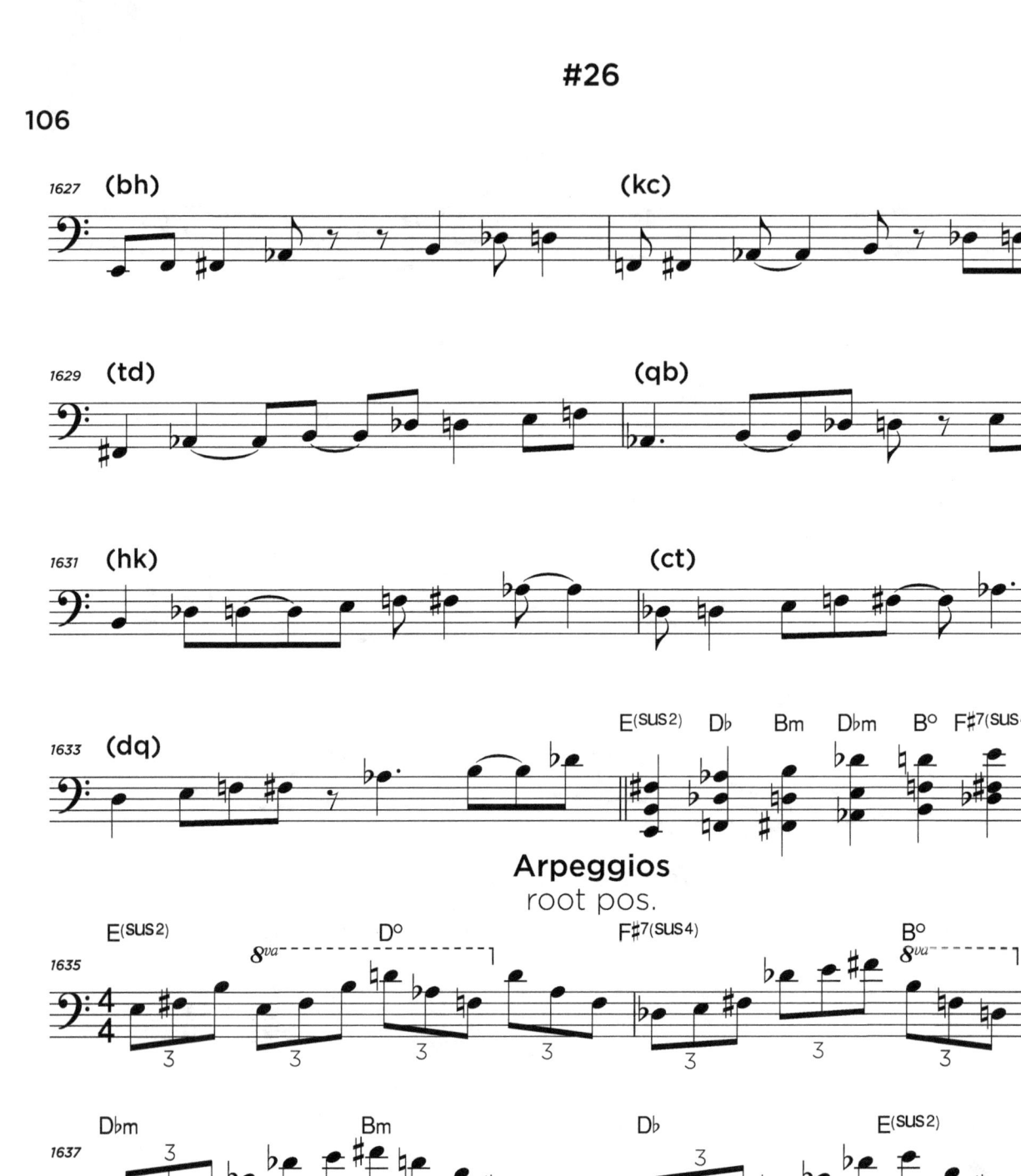

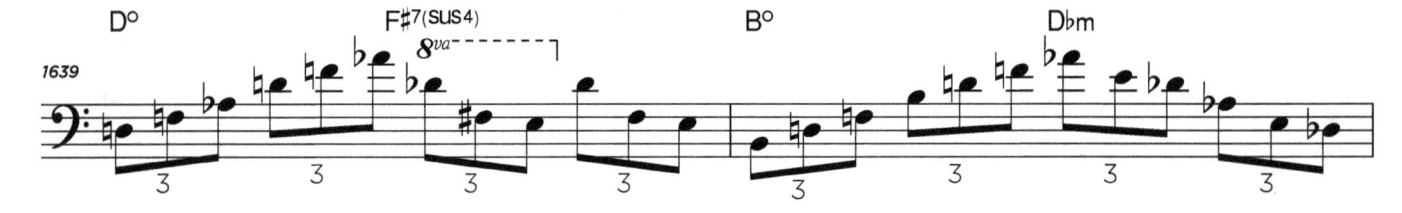

107

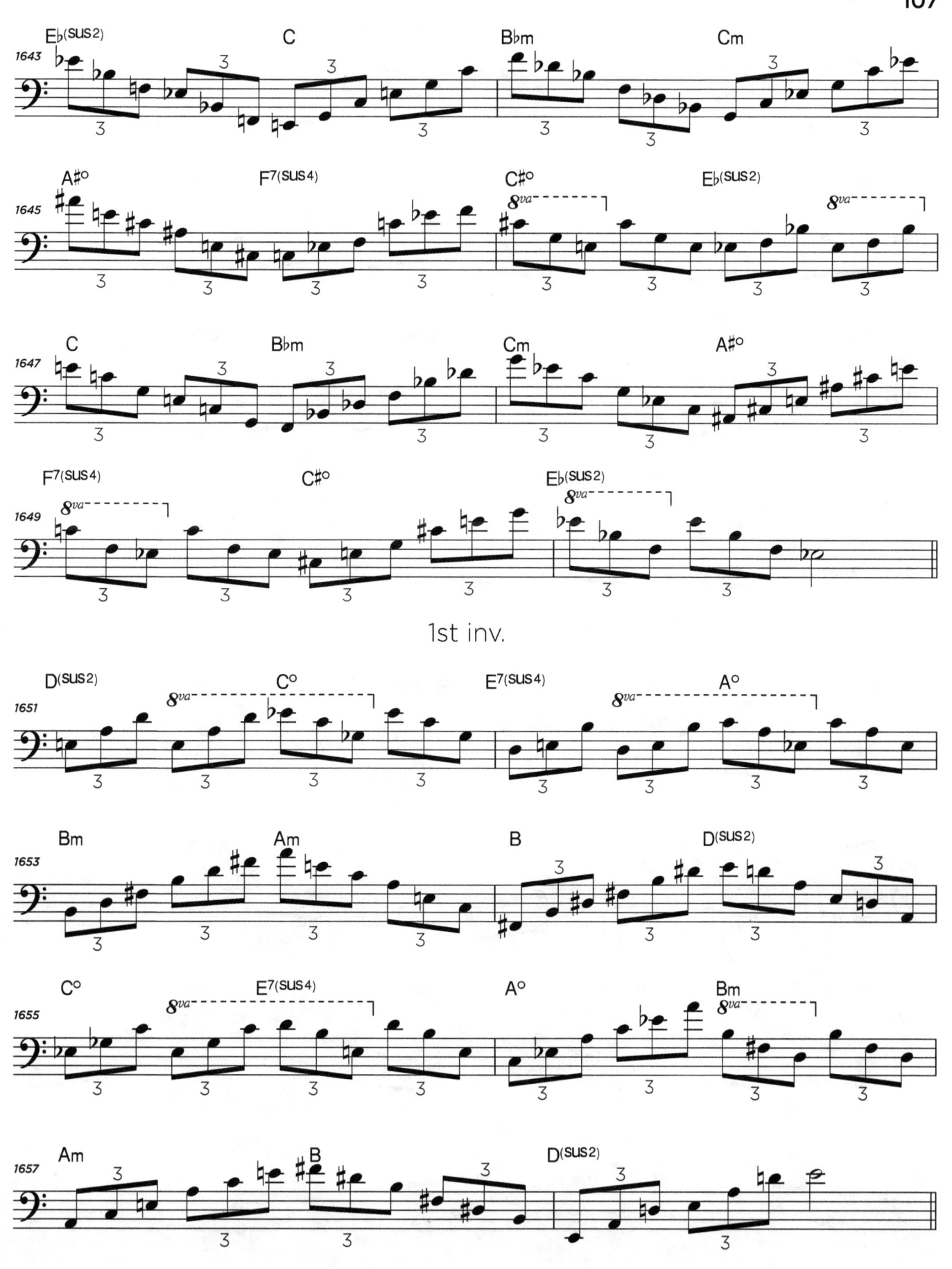

108

Voice Leading

© 2017 by Felix Pastorius

#27

1707
Ab7(SUS4) Em Ab7 G+
1709
Ab+ B C Ab7(SUS4)
8va
1711
Em Ab7 G+ Ab+
1713
B C Ab7(SUS4)
8va
8va

1st inv.

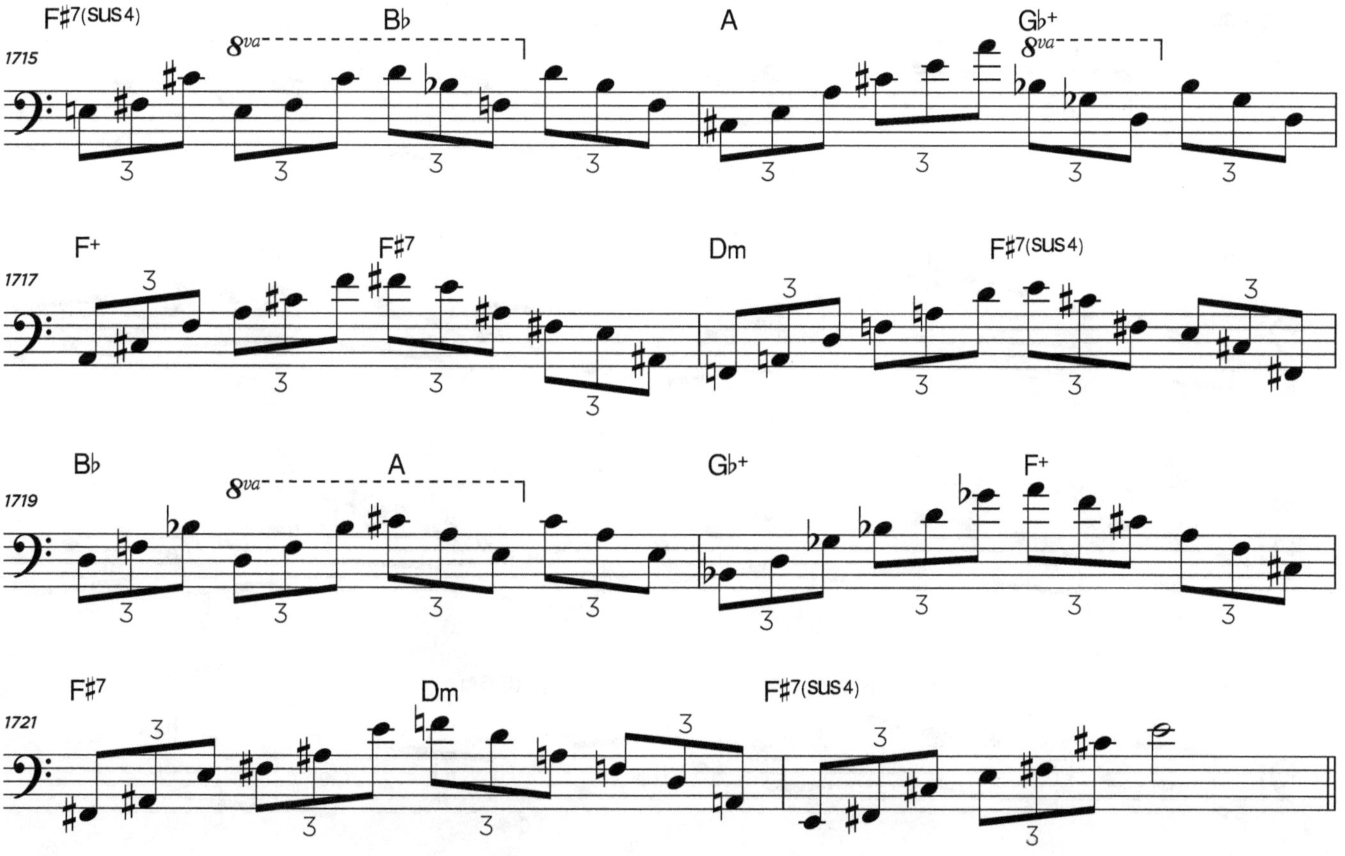
1715
F#7(SUS4) Bb A Gb+
8va
8va
1717
F+ F#7 Dm F#7(SUS4)
1719
Bb A Gb+ F+
8va
1721
F#7 Dm F#7(SUS4)

1723
F7(SUS4)
C♯m
F7
E+
1725
F+
A♭
A
F7(SUS4)
1727
C♯m
F7
E+
F+
1729
A♭
A
F7(SUS4)

2nd inv.

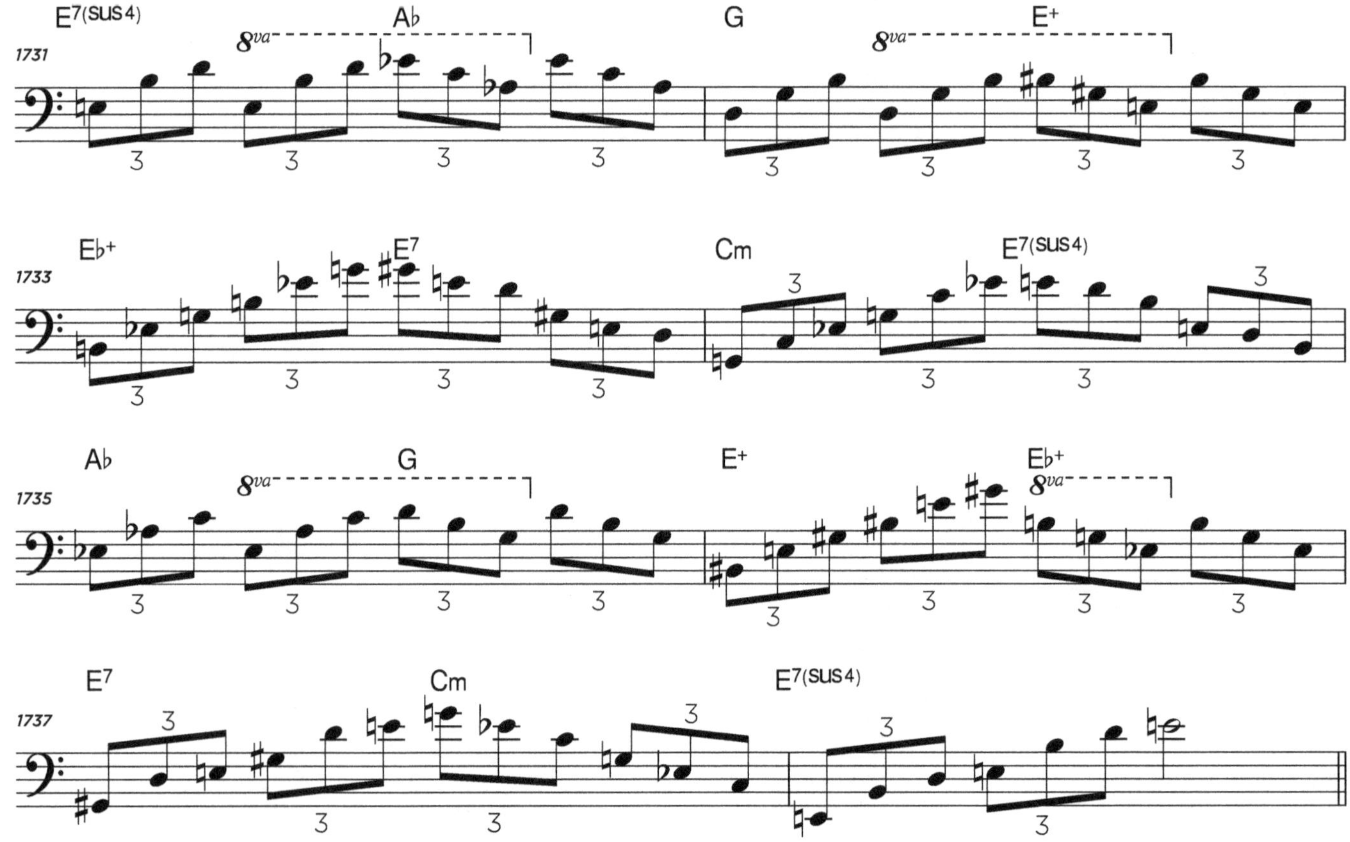
1731
E7(SUS4)
A♭
G
E+
1733
E♭+
E7
Cm
E7(SUS4)
1735
A♭
G
E+
E♭+
1737
E7
Cm
E7(SUS4)

Voice Leading

#28

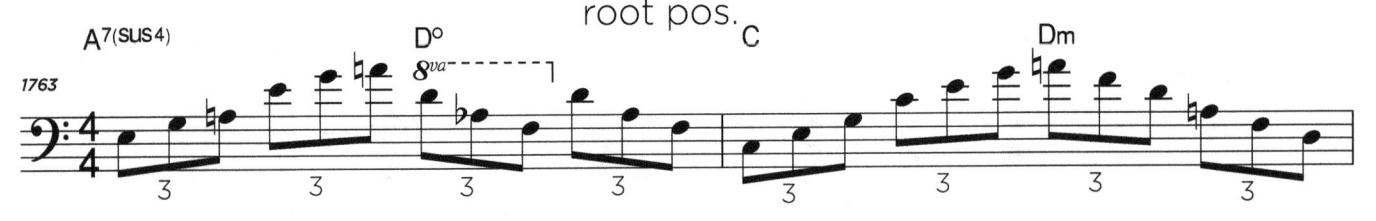

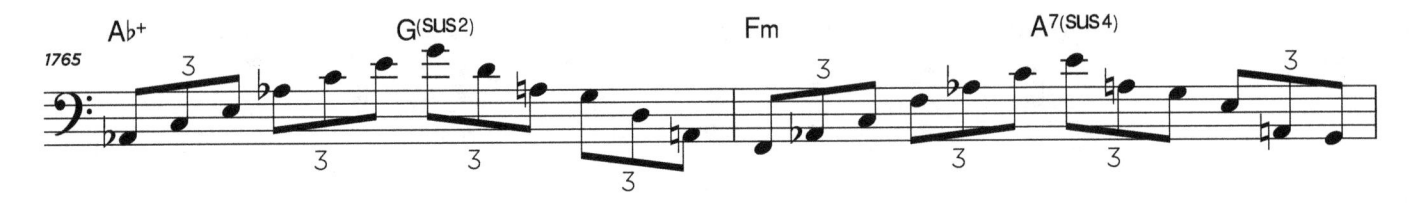

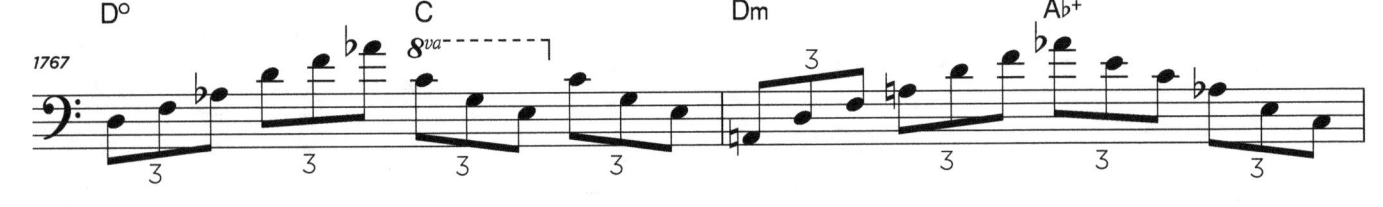

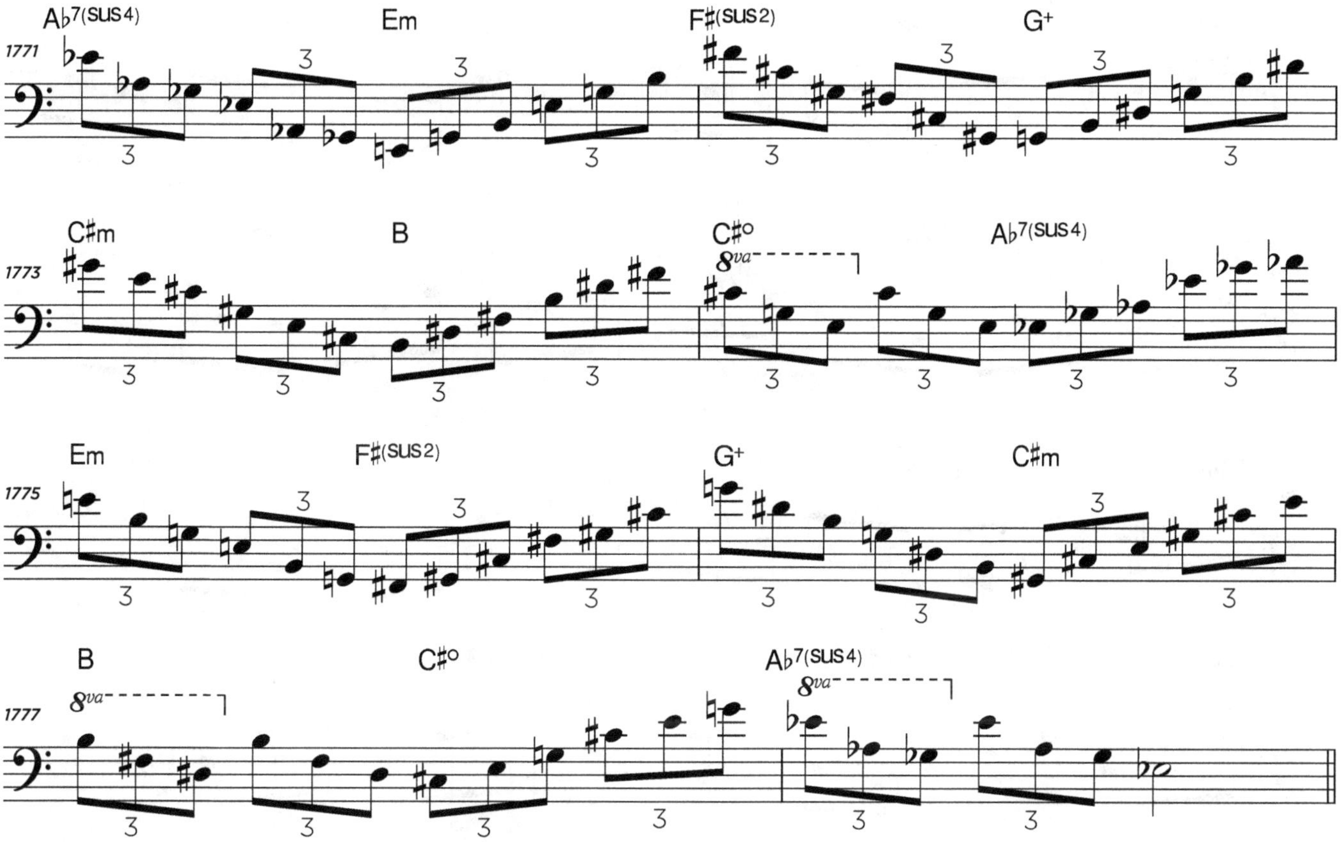
1771
A♭7(SUS4)
Em
F♯(SUS2)
G+
1773
C♯m
B
C♯o
A♭7(SUS4)
1775
Em
F♯(SUS2)
G+
C♯m
1777
B
C♯o
A♭7(SUS4)

1st inv.

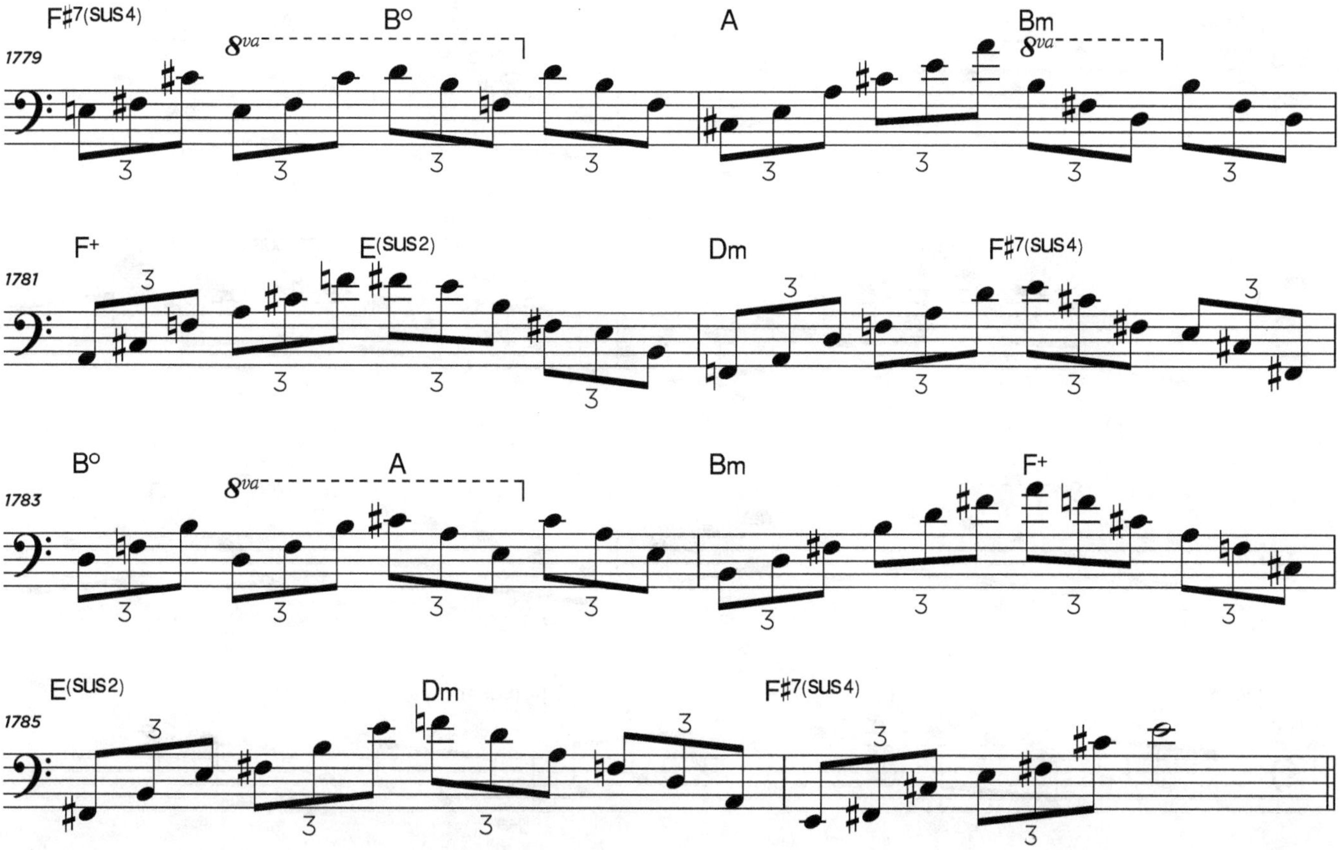
1779
F♯7(SUS4)
Bo
A
Bm
1781
F+
E(SUS2)
Dm
F♯7(SUS4)
1783
Bo
A
Bm
F+
1785
E(SUS2)
Dm
F♯7(SUS4)

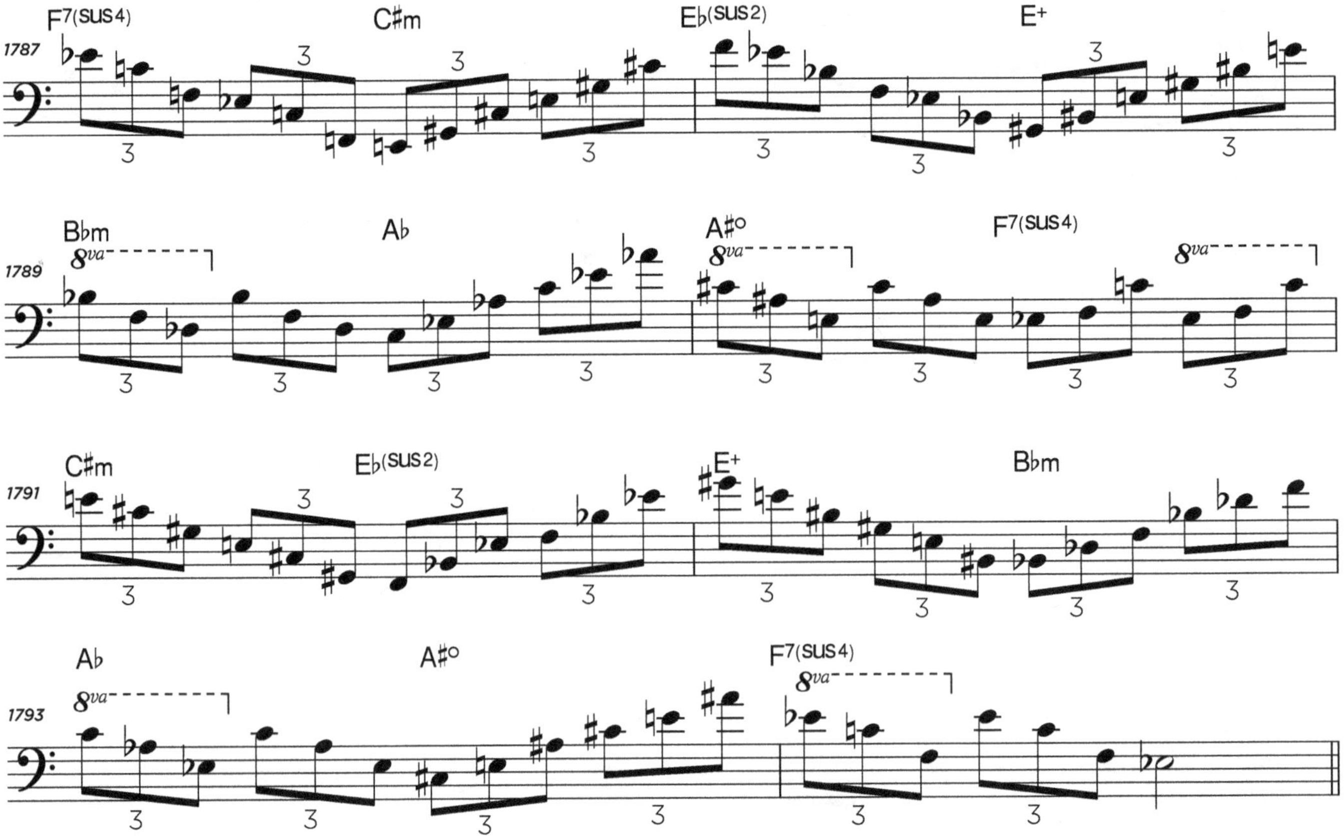
1787
F7(SUS4) C♯m E♭(SUS2) E+
1789
B♭m A♭ A♯o F7(SUS4)
1791
C♯m E♭(SUS2) E+ B♭m
1793
A♭ A♯o F7(SUS4)

2nd inv.

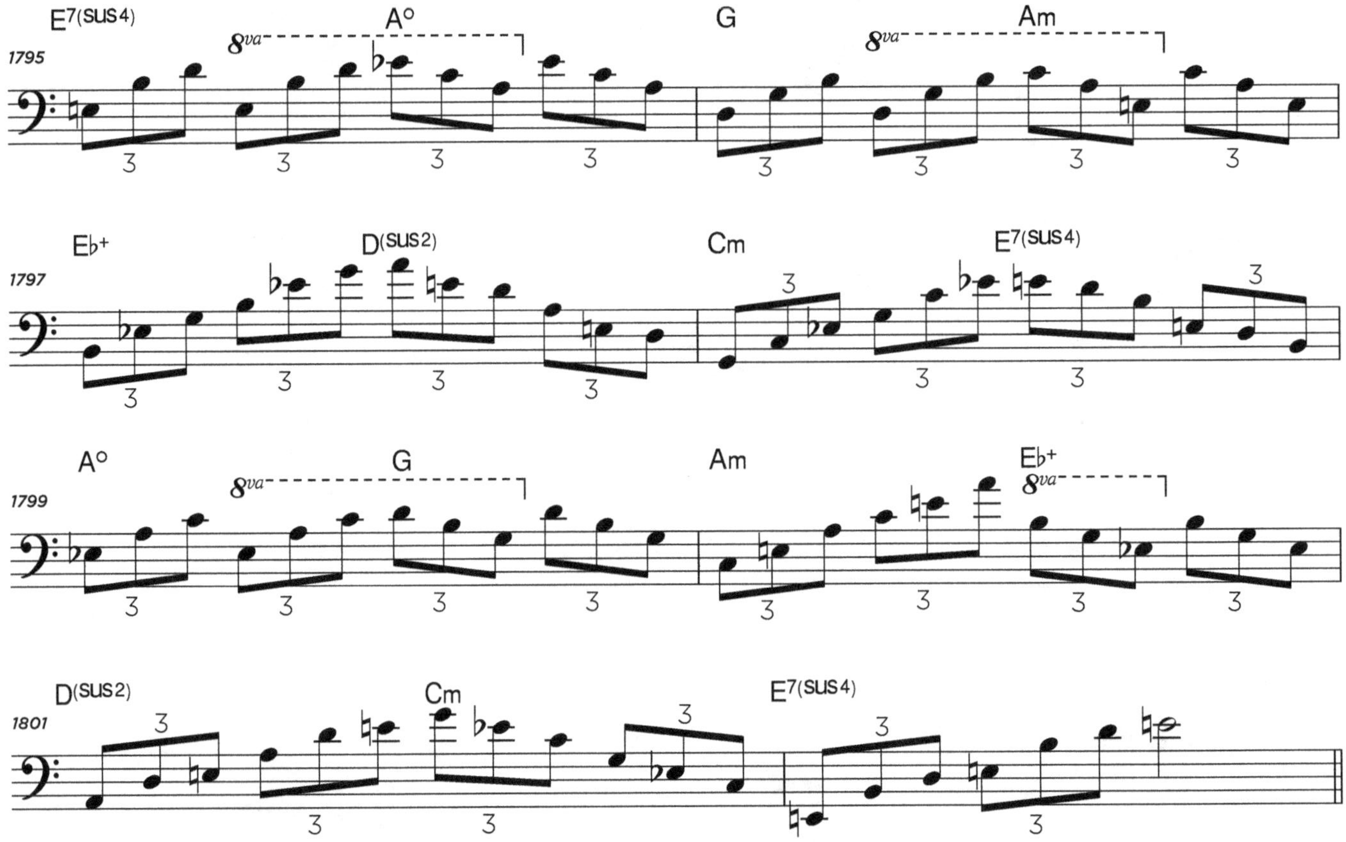
1795
E7(SUS4) Ao G Am
1797
E♭+ D(SUS2) Cm E7(SUS4)
1799
Ao G Am E♭+
1801
D(SUS2) Cm E7(SUS4)

Voice Leading

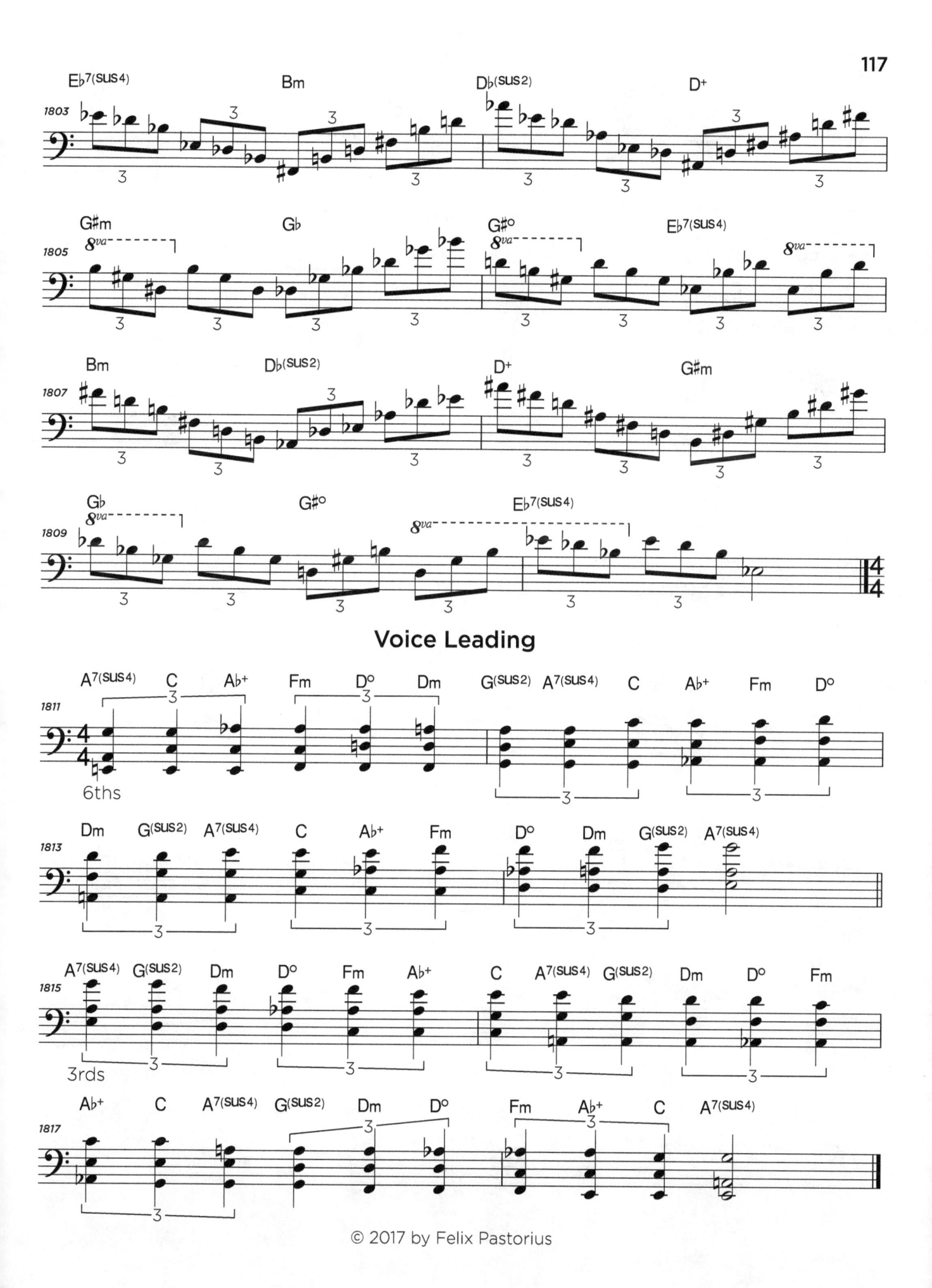

#29

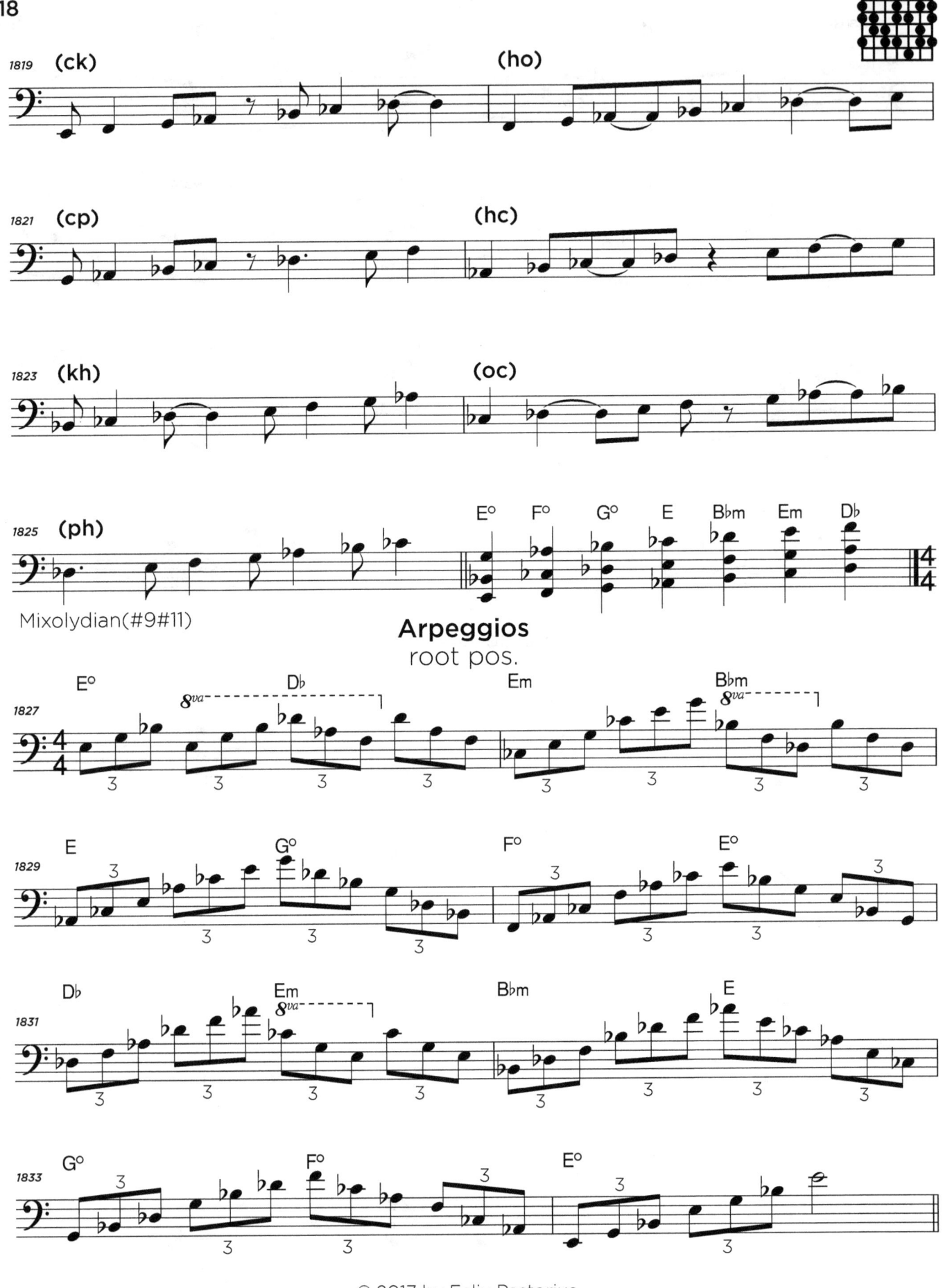

119

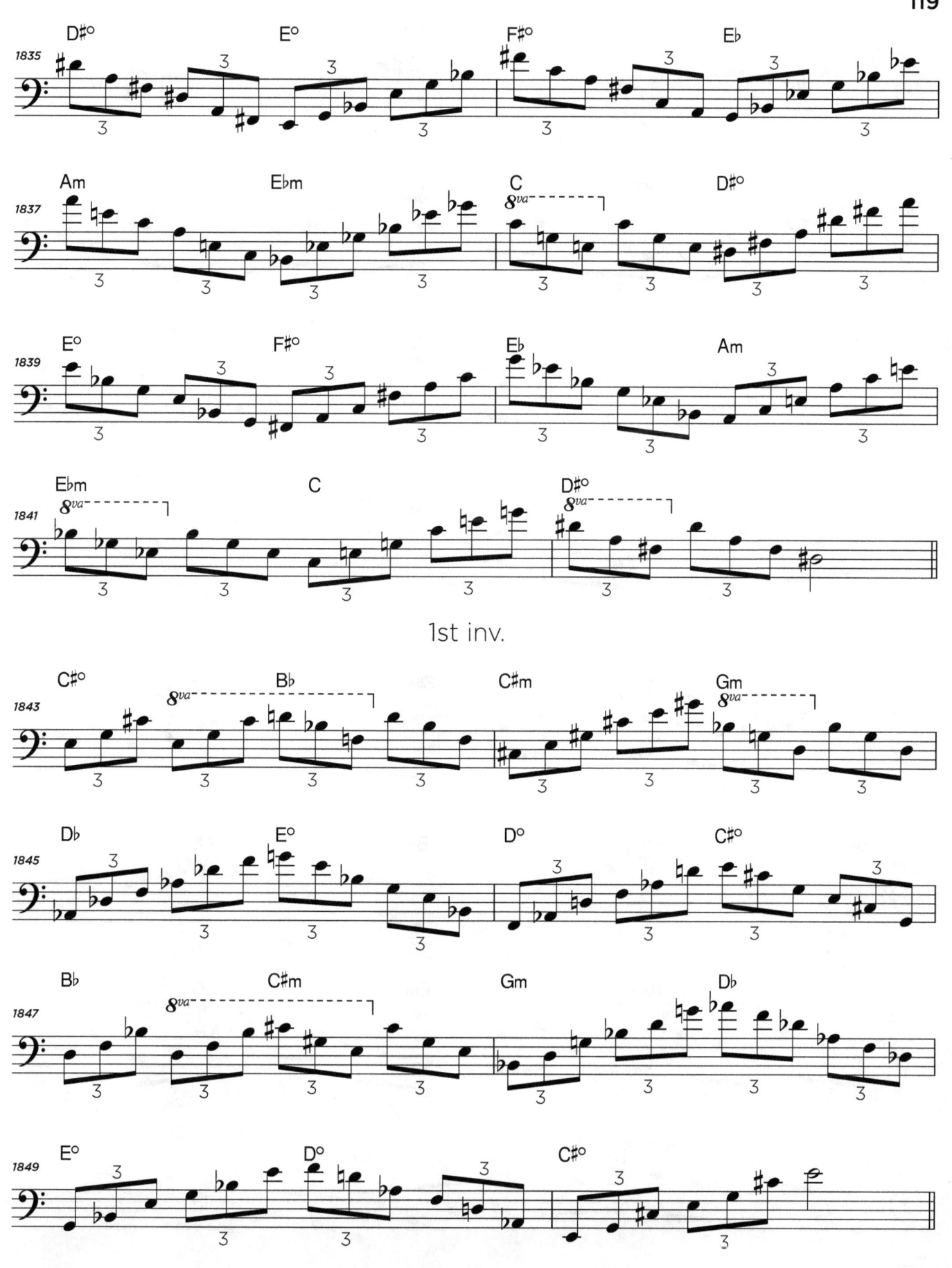

120

Voice Leading

#30

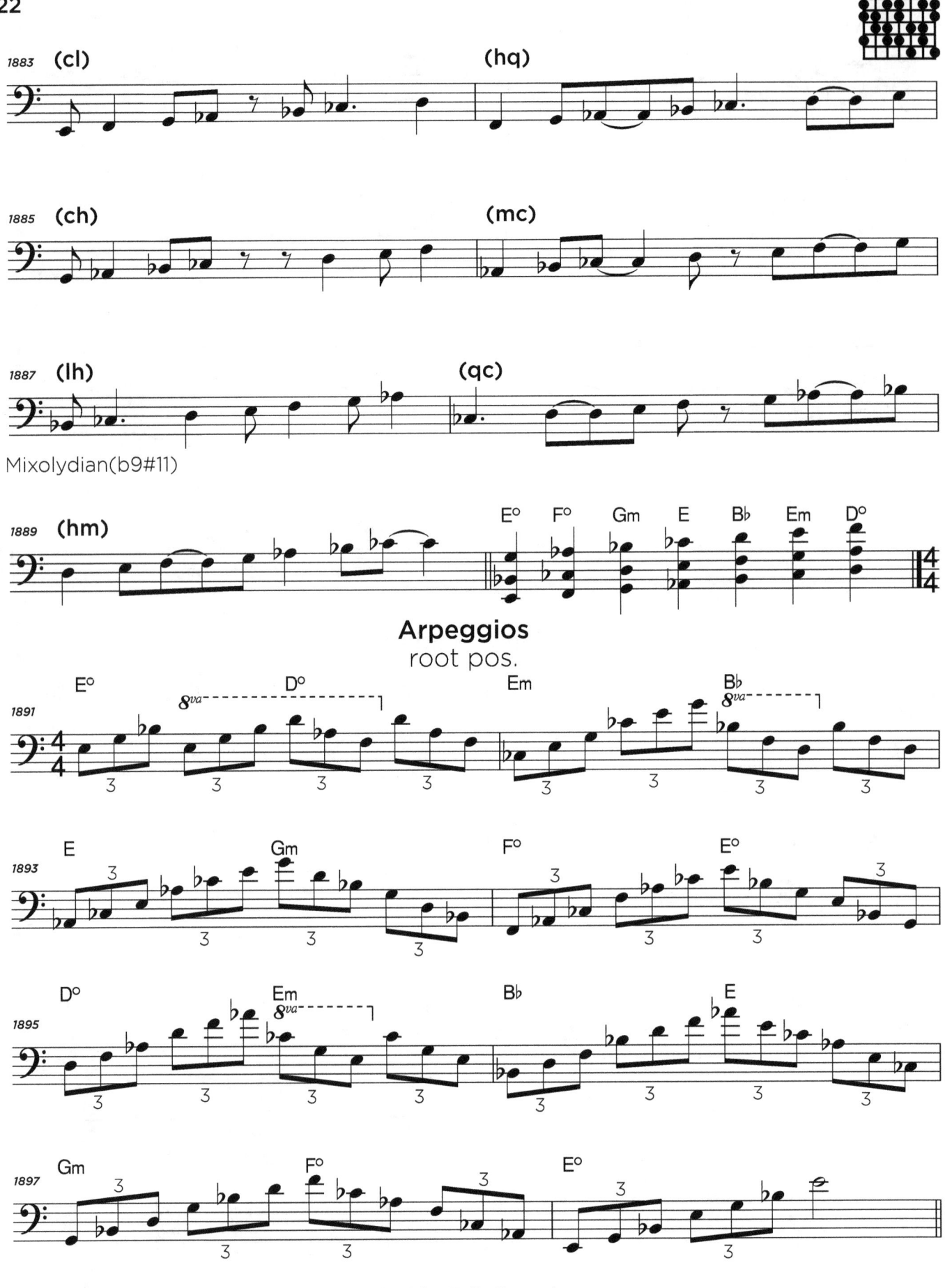

Mixolydian(b9#11)

1899
D♯o
E°
F♯m
E♭
1901
A
E♭m
C♯o
D♯o
1903
E°
F♯m
E♭
A
1905
E♭m
C♯o
D♯o
8va

1st inv.

1907
C♯o
B°
C♯m
G
1909
D♭
Em
D°
C♯o
1911
B°
C♯m
G
D♭
1913
Em
D°
C♯o
8va

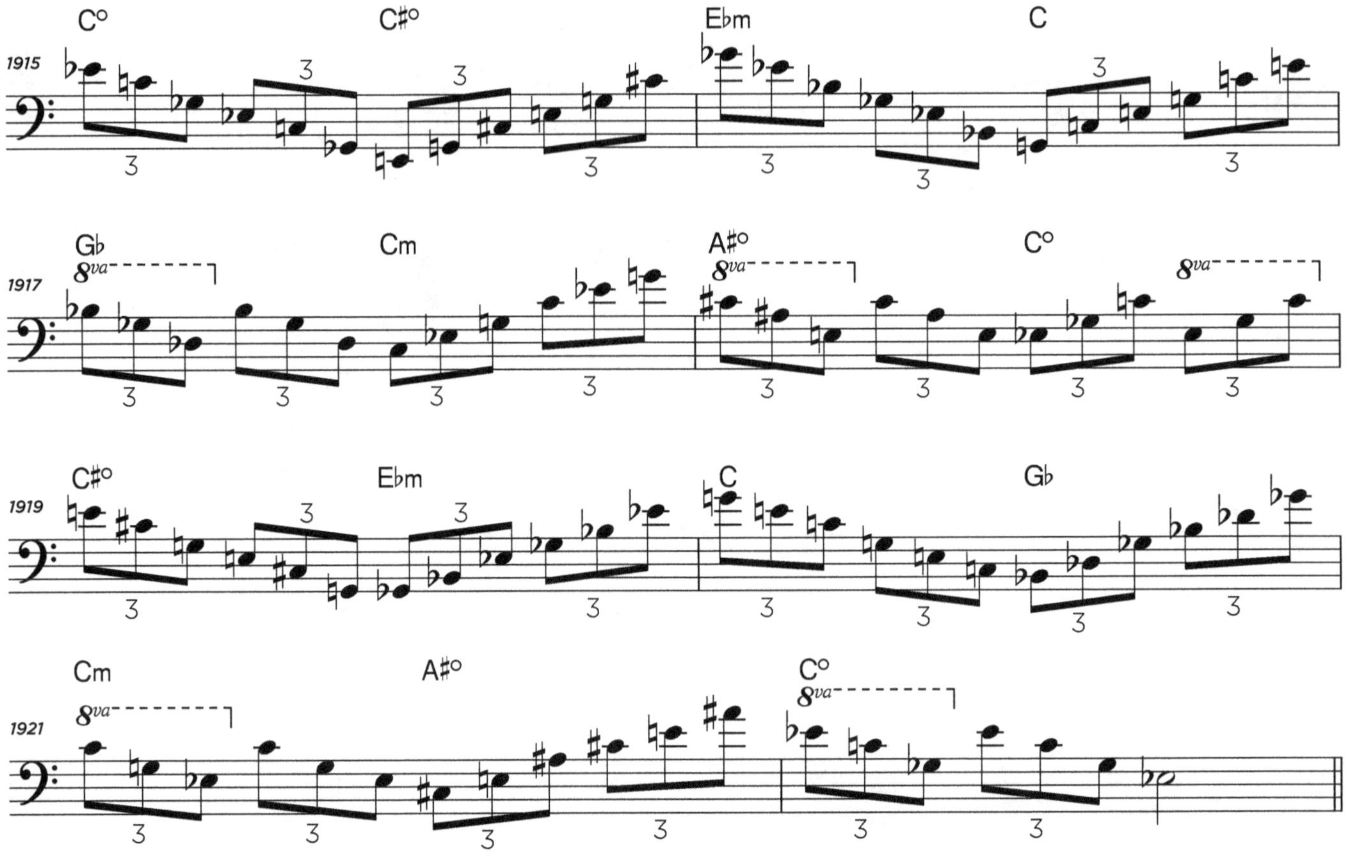
1915
C°
C♯°
E♭m
C
1917
G♭
8va
Cm
A♯°
8va
C°
8va
1919
C♯°
E♭m
C
G♭
1921
Cm
8va
A♯°
C°
8va

2nd inv.

1923
A♯°
8va
G♯°
B♭m
8va
E
1925
B♭
C♯m
B°
A♯°
1927
G♯°
8va
B♭m
E
B♭
8va
1929
C♯m
B°
A♯°

Voice Leading

#31

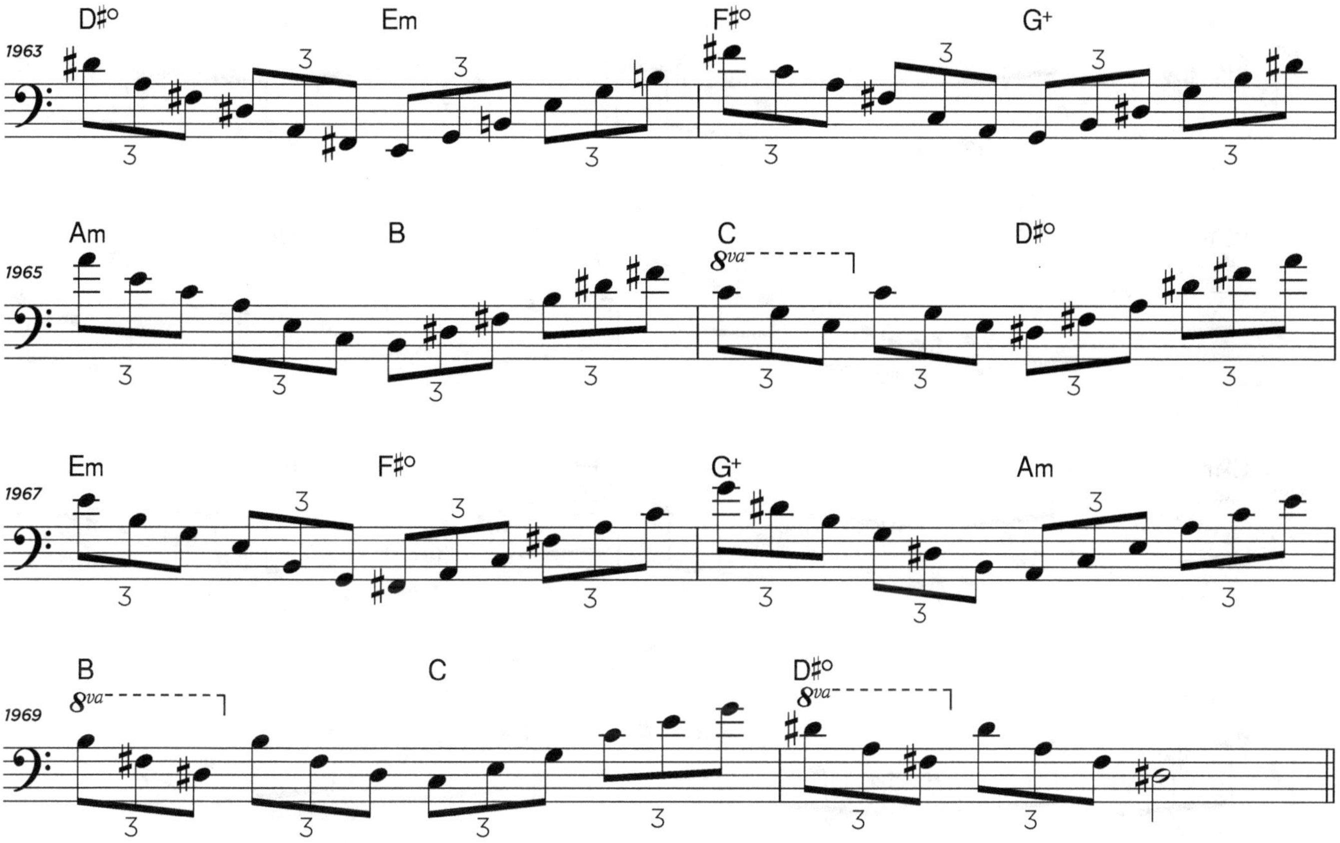
D♯o
Em
F♯o
G+
1963
Am
B
C
D♯o
1965
Em
F♯o
G+
Am
1967
B
C
D♯o
1969

1st inv.

C♯o
B♭
A
Gm
1971
F+
Eo
Dm
C♯o
1973
B♭
A
Gm
F+
1975
Eo
Dm
C♯o
1977

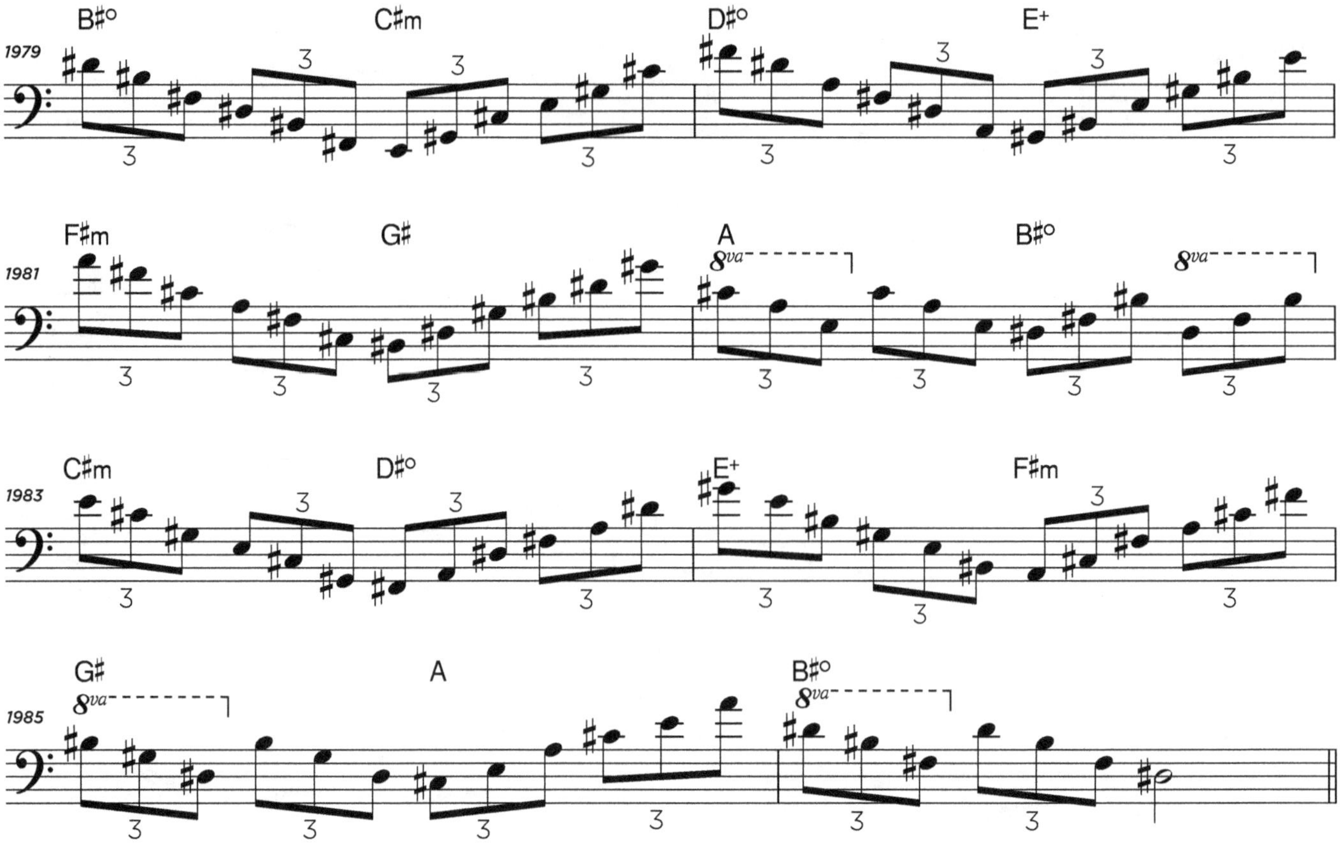
B♯o
C♯m
D♯o
E+
F♯m
G♯
A
B♯o
C♯m
D♯o
E+
F♯m
G♯
A
B♯o
1979
1981
1983
1985
8va

2nd inv.

A♯o
G
F♯
Em
D+
C♯o
Bm
A♯o
G
F♯
Em
D+
C♯o
Bm
A♯o
1987
1989
1991
1993
8va

Voice Leading

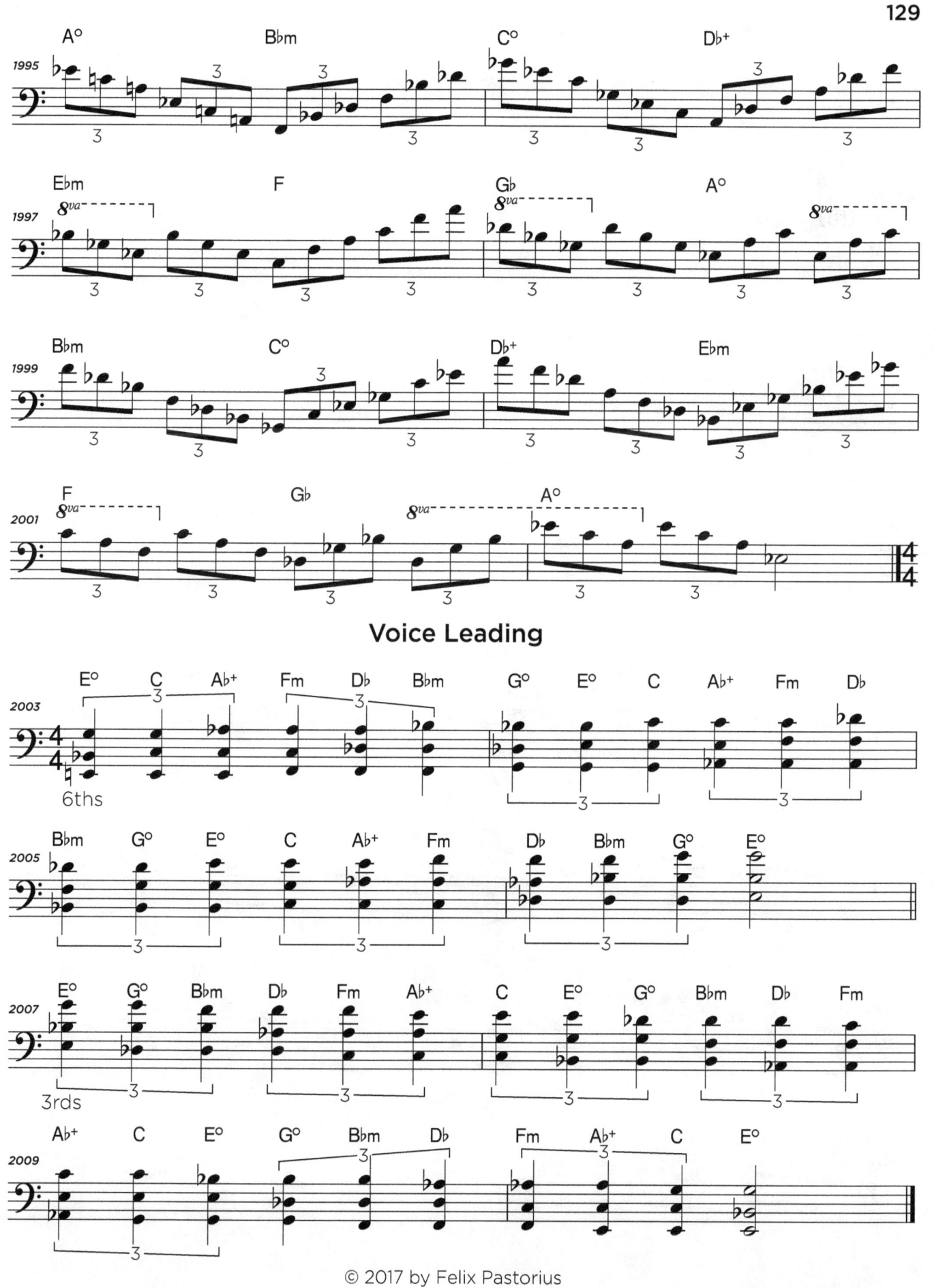

#32

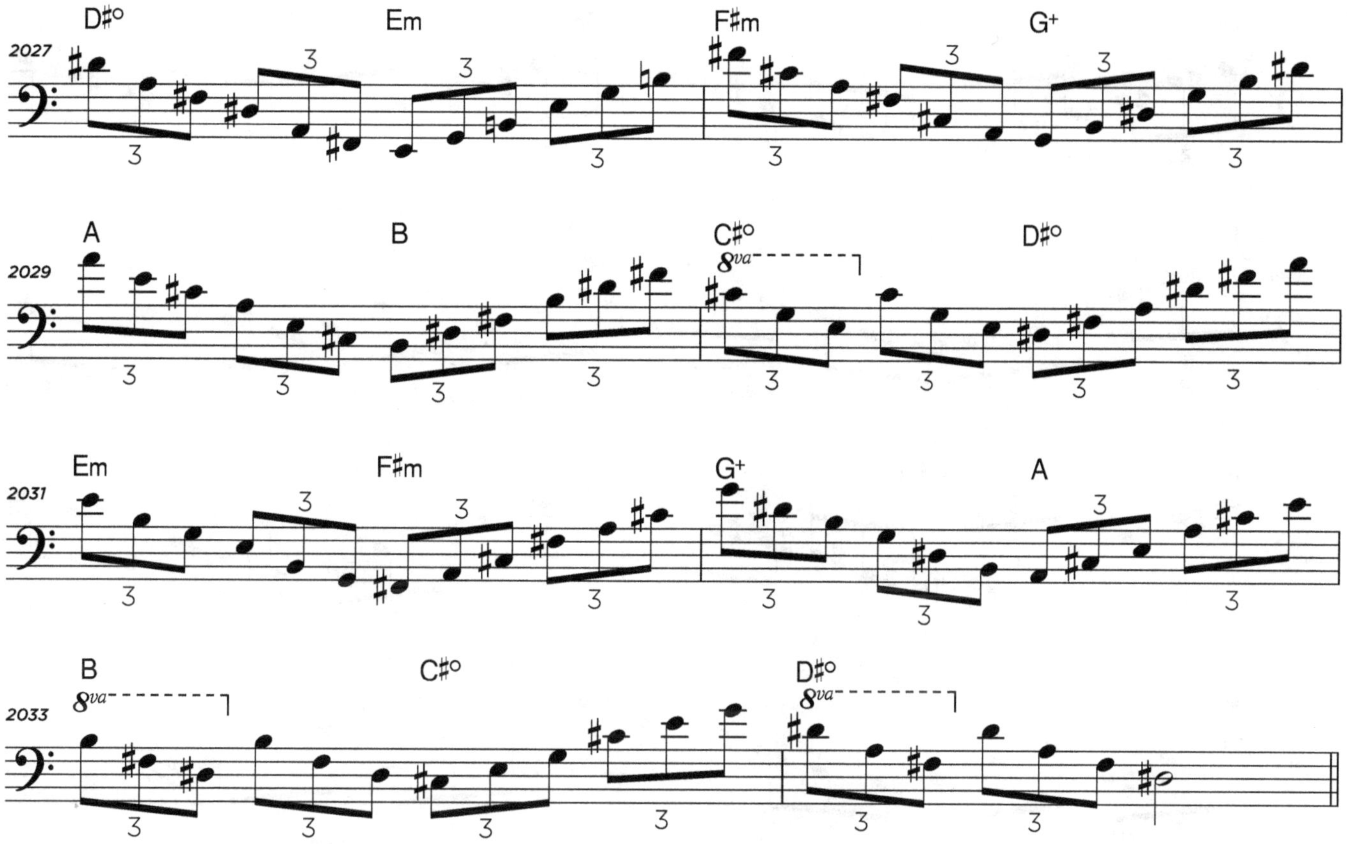
2027
D♯o
Em
F♯m
G+
2029
A
B
C♯o
D♯o
2031
Em
F♯m
G+
A
2033
B
C♯o
D♯o

1st inv.

2035
C♯o
Bo
A
G
2037
F+
Em
Dm
C♯o
2039
Bo
A
G
F+
2041
Em
Dm
C♯o

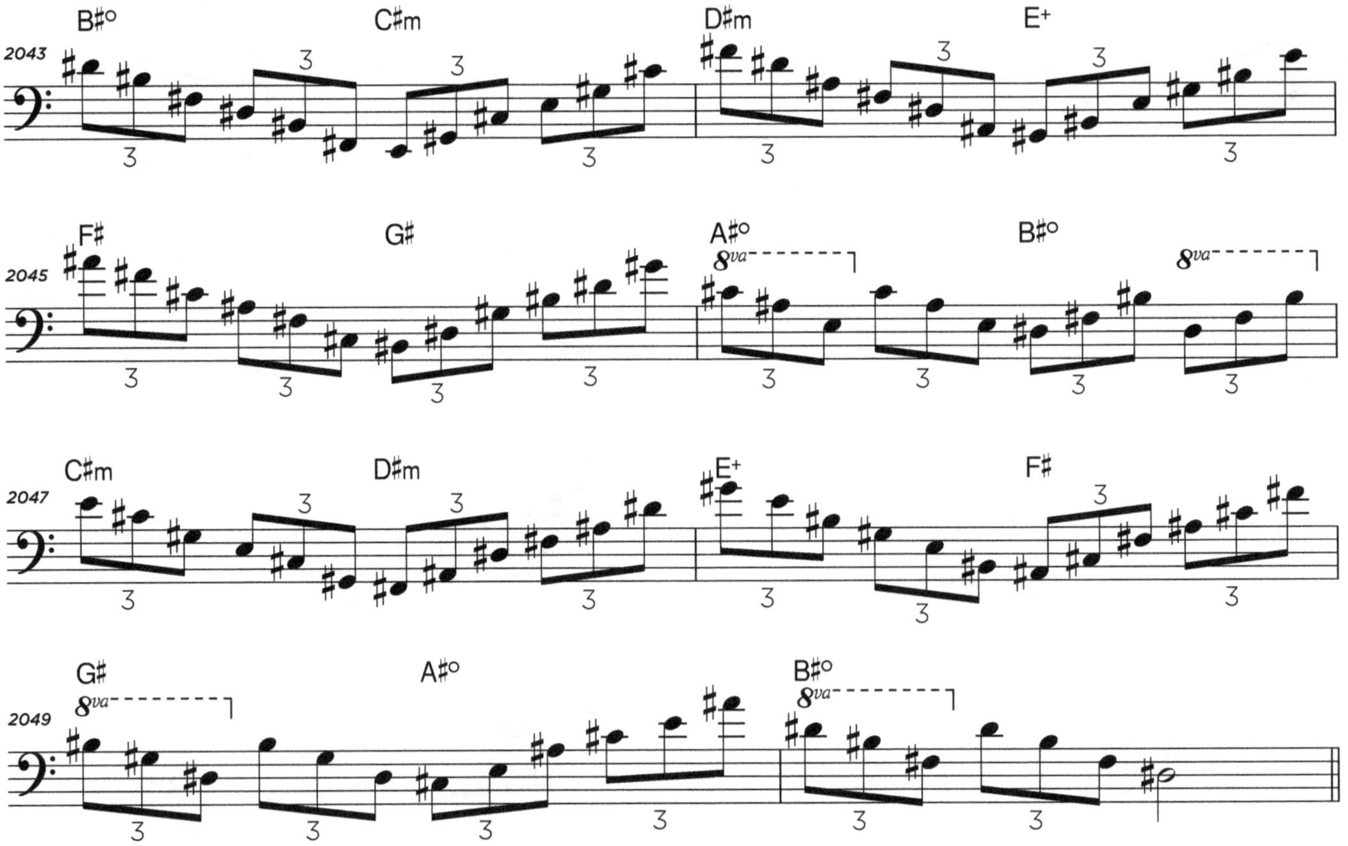
2043
B♯o
C♯m
D♯m
E+
2045
F♯
G♯
A♯o
8va
B♯o
8va
2047
C♯m
D♯m
E+
F♯
2049
G♯
8va
A♯o
B♯o
8va

2nd inv.

2051
A♯o
8va
G♯o
F♯
E
8va
2053
D+
C♯m
Bm
A♯o
2055
G♯o
8va
F♯
E
D+
2057
C♯m
Bm
A♯o

Voice Leading

#33

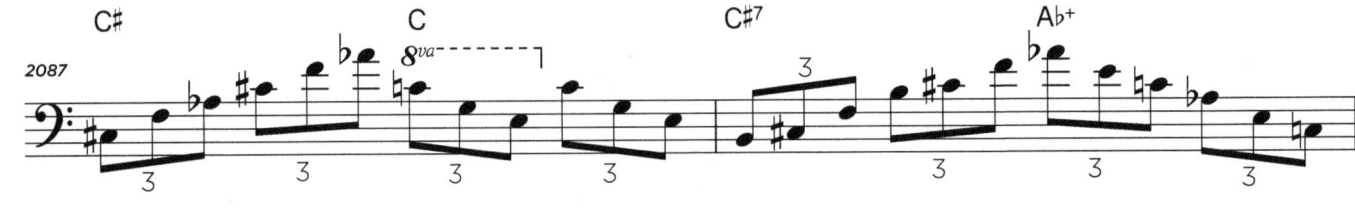

2091
Ebm
Em
Gb(b5)
G+
2093
C7
B
C
Ebm
8va
2095
Em
Gb(b5)
G+
C7
2097
B
C
Ebm
8va

1st inv.

2099
C#m
Bb
A
Bb7
8va
2101
F+
E(b5)
Dm
C#m
2103
Bb
A
Bb7
F+
8va
2105
E(b5)
Dm
C#m

Cm
C♯m
E♭(♭5)
E+
2107
A7
A♭
A
Cm
2109
C♯m
E♭(♭5)
E+
A7
2111
A♭
A
Cm
2113

2nd inv.

Am
G♭
F
F♯7
2115
D♭+
C(♭5)
B♭m
Am
2117
G♭
F
F♯7
D♭+
2119
C(♭5)
B♭m
Am
2121

Voice Leading

© 2017 by Felix Pastorius

#34

138

Major(Harmonic)

Arpeggios
root pos.

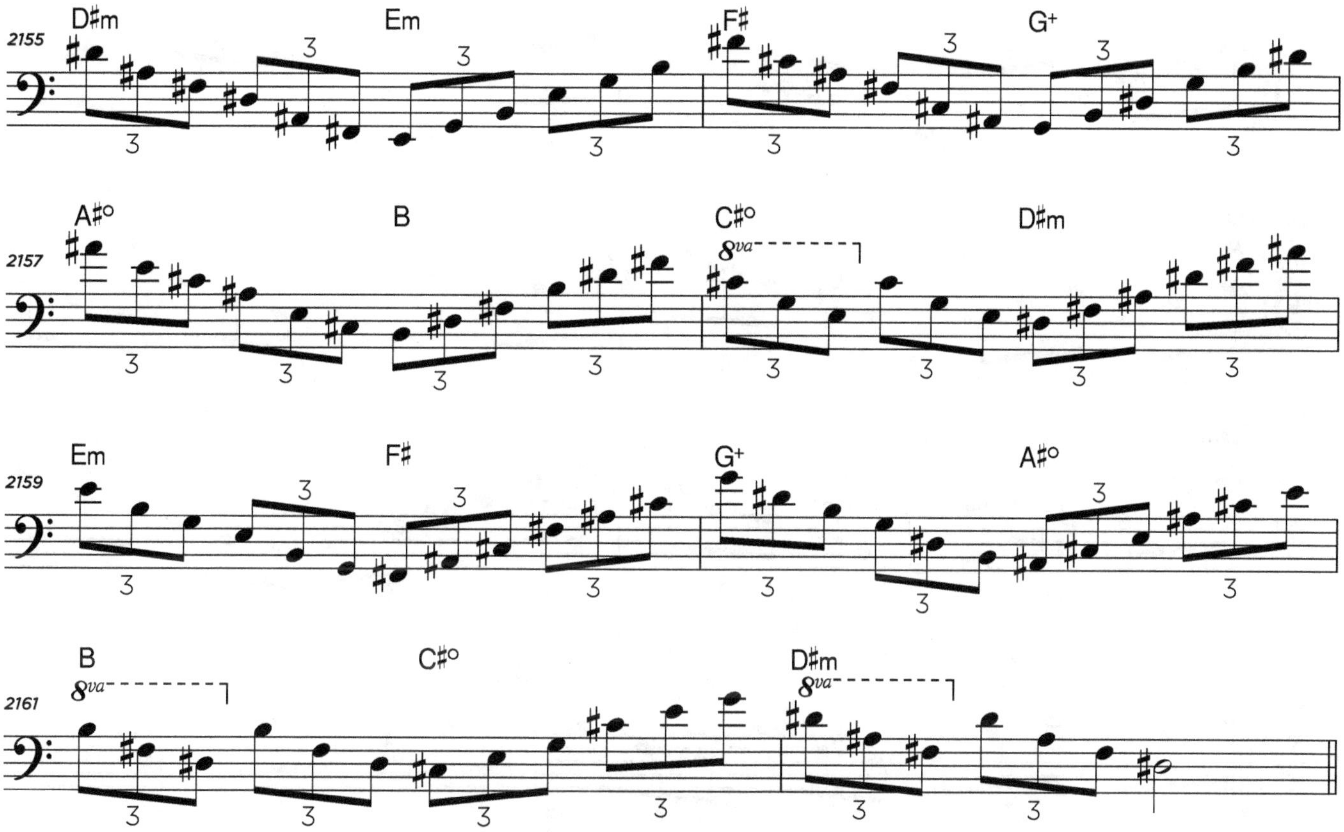
2155
D♯m
Em
F♯
G+
2157
A♯°
B
C♯°
8va
D♯m
2159
Em
F♯
G+
A♯°
2161
B
8va
C♯°
D♯m
8va

1st inv.

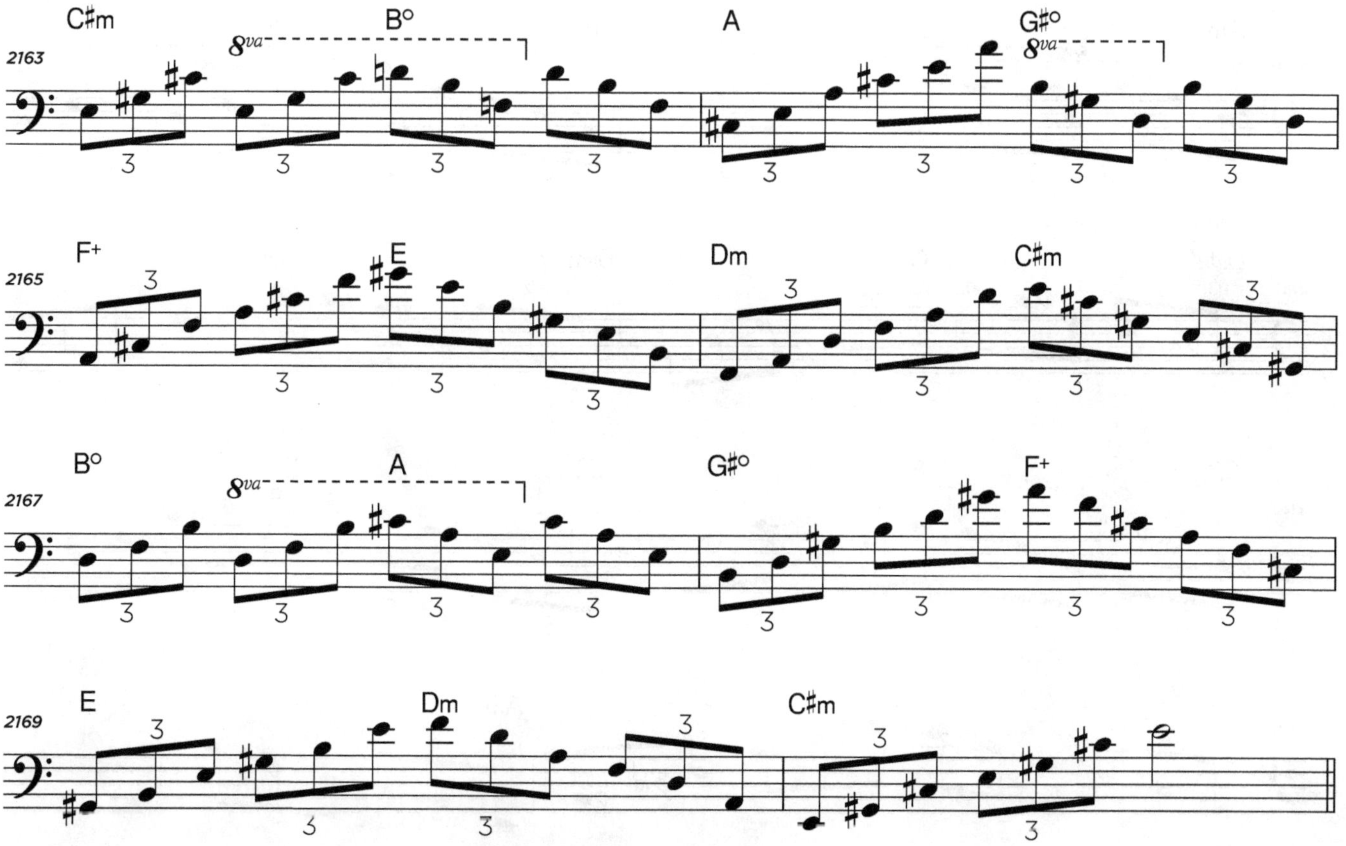
2163
C♯m
8va
B°
A
G♯°
8va
2165
F+
E
Dm
C♯m
2167
B°
8va
A
G♯°
F+
2169
E
Dm
C♯m

Cm
Dbm
Eb
Fb+
2171
G°
Ab
Bb°
Cm
2173
Dbm
Eb
Fb+
G°
2175
Ab
Bb°
Cm
2177

2nd inv.

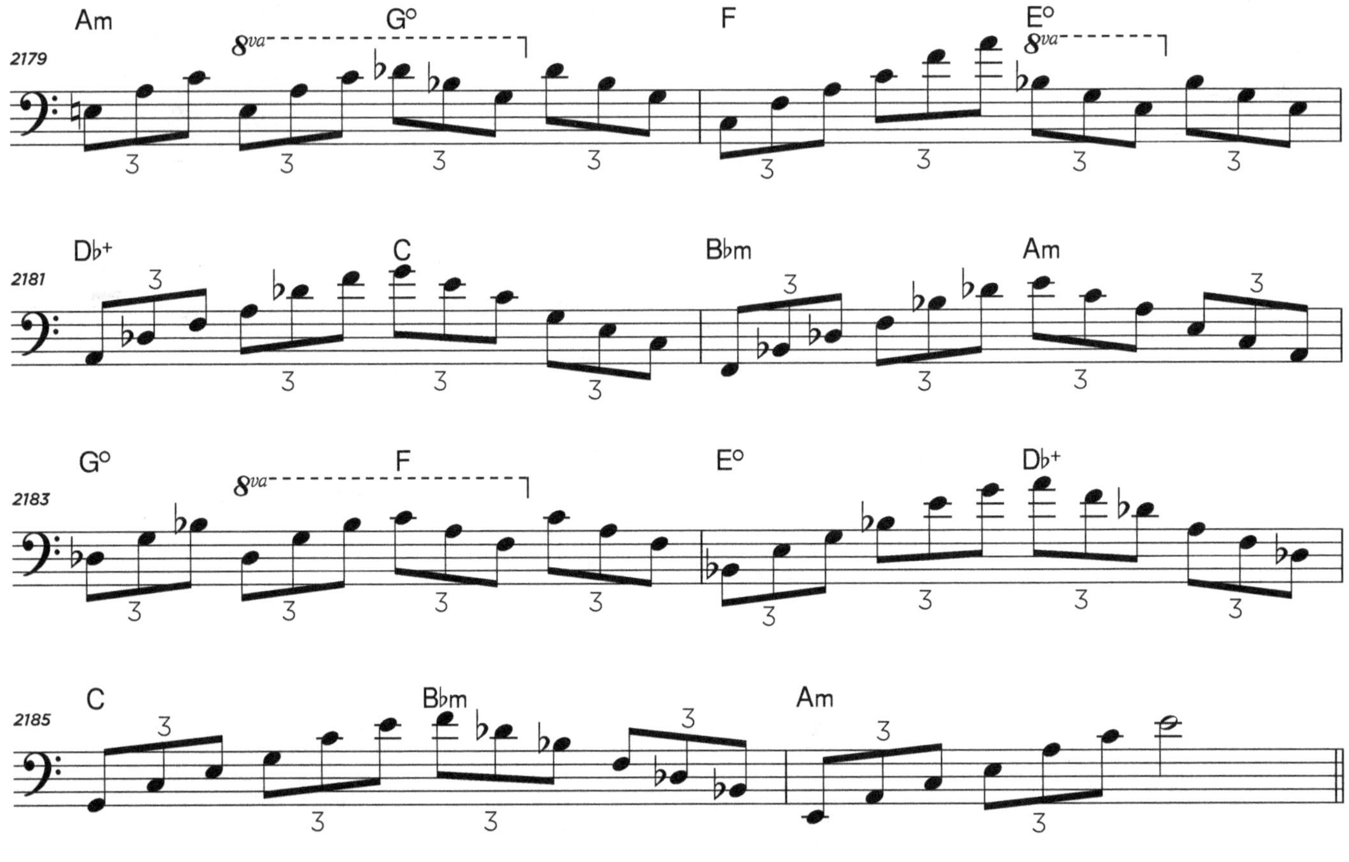
Am
G°
F
E°
2179
Db+
C
Bbm
Am
2181
G°
F
E°
Db+
2183
C
Bbm
Am
2185

Voice Leading

#35

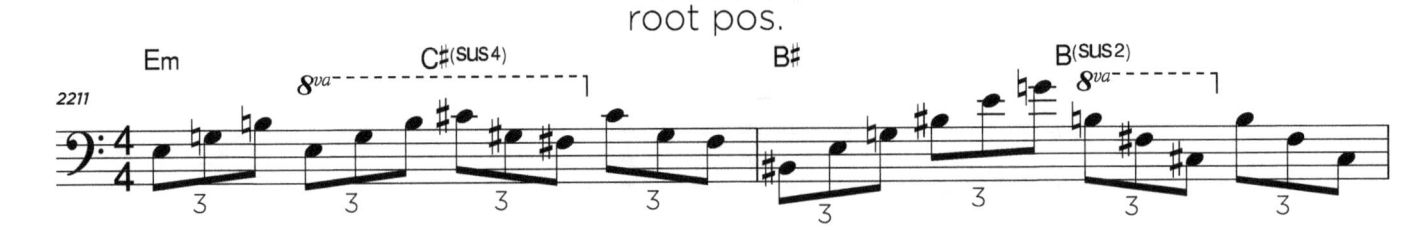

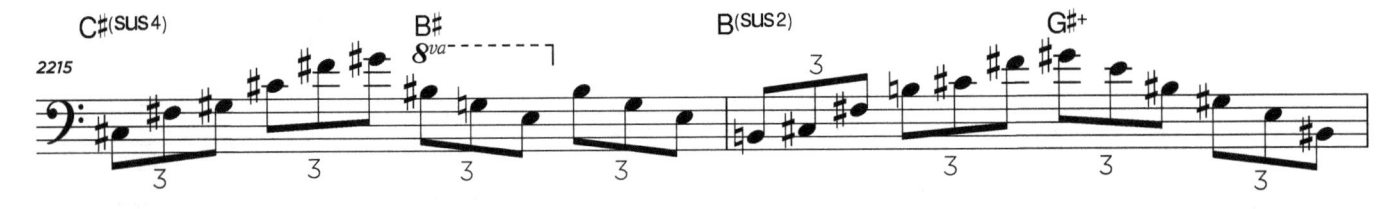

143

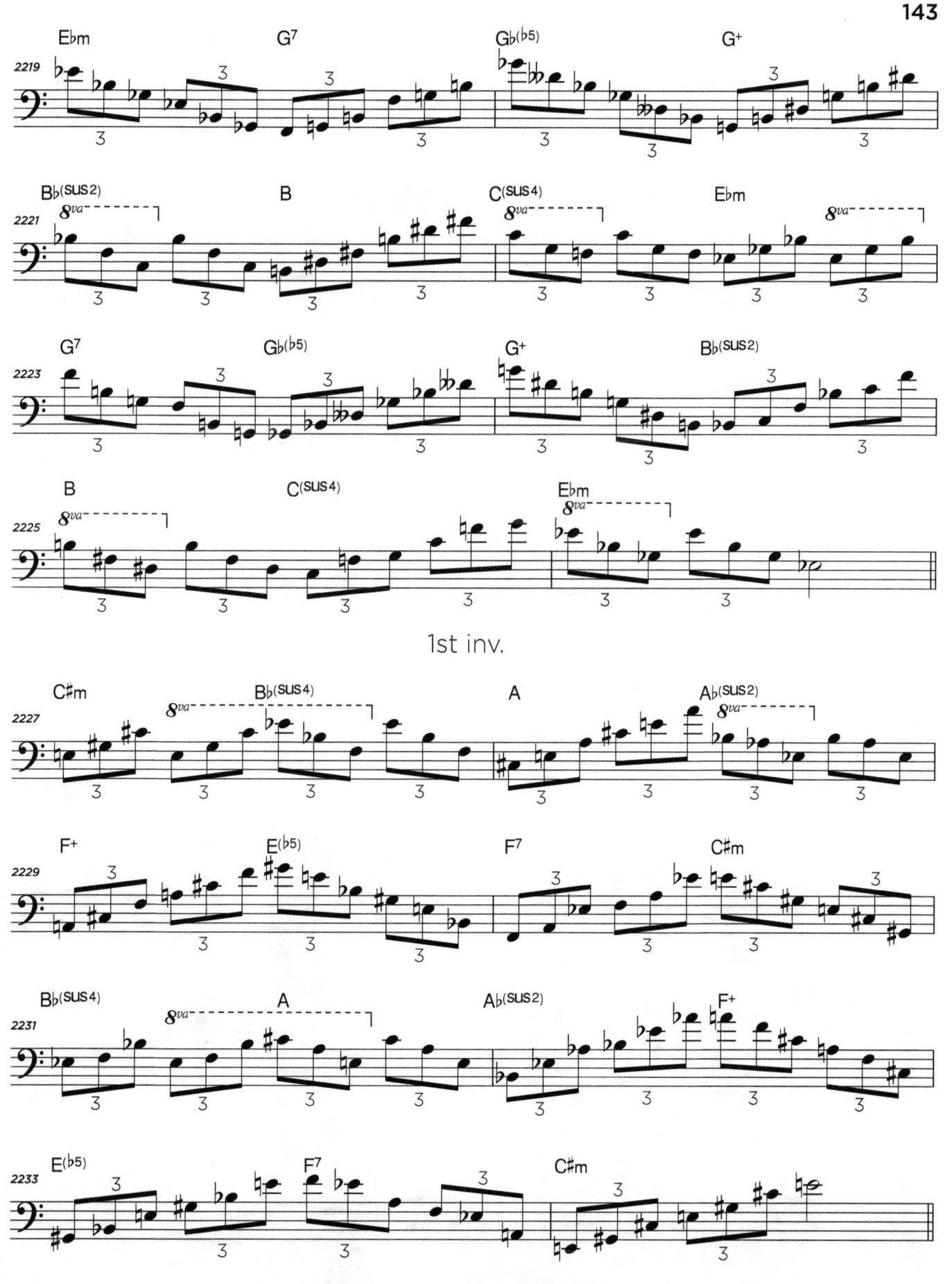

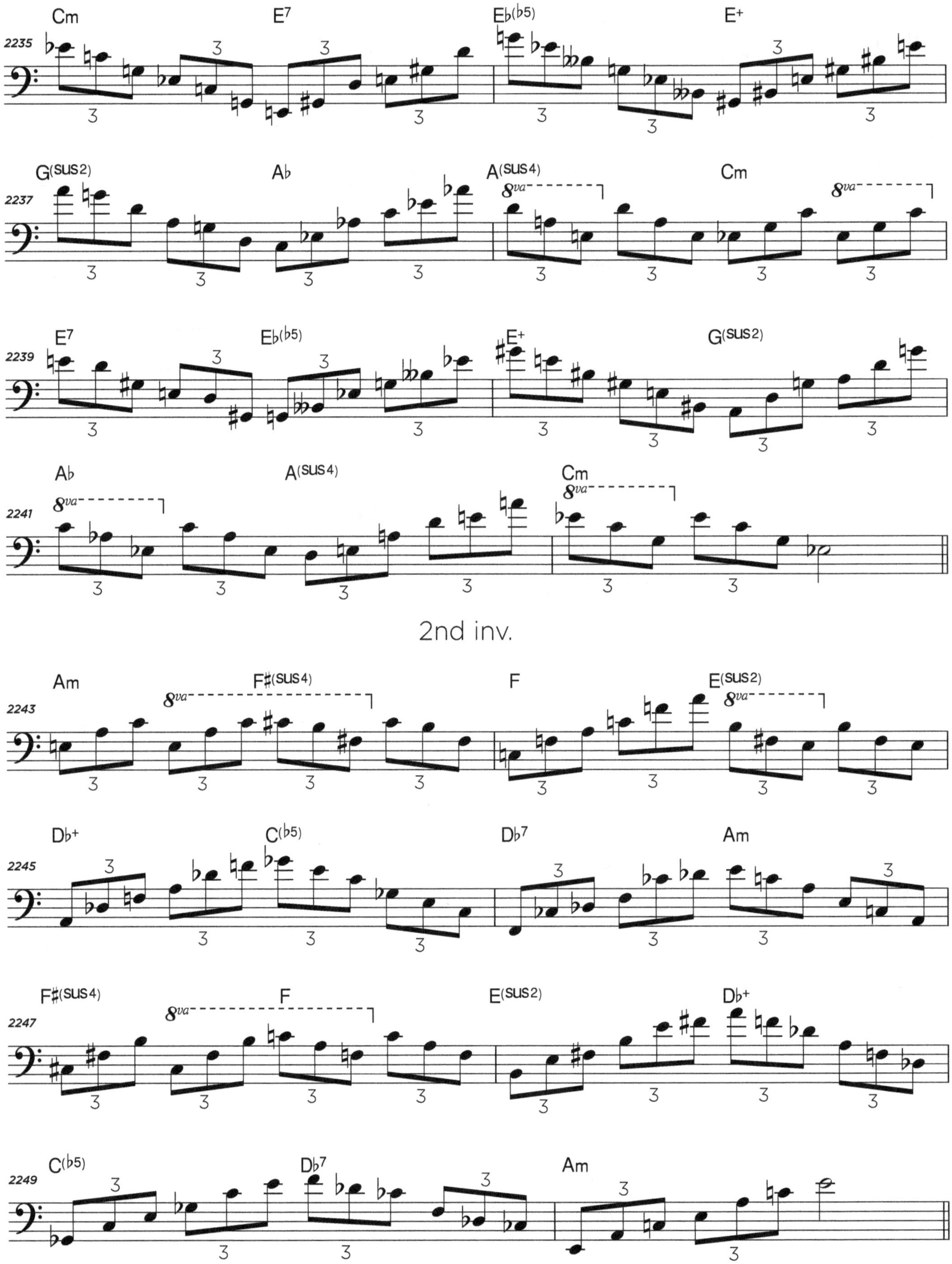
2235
Cm E7 Eb(b5) E+
2237
G(sus2) Ab A(sus4) Cm
8va
2239
E7 Eb(b5) E+ G(sus2)
2241
Ab A(sus4) Cm
8va
2nd inv.
2243
Am F#(sus4) F E(sus2)
8va
2245
Db+ C(b5) Db7 Am
2247
F#(sus4) F E(sus2) Db+
8va
2249
C(b5) Db7 Am

Voice Leading

#36

2267 (df)
(en)
2269 (gi)
(pd)
2271 (fe)
(ng)
2273 (ip)
Em G♯7 G G♯+ Bm B♯ D(♭5)
Arpeggios
root pos.
2275 Em D(♭5) B♯ Bm
2277 G♯+ G G♯7 Em
2279 D(♭5) B♯ Bm G♯+
2281 G G♯7 Em

2283
E♭m
G7
G♭
G+
2285
B♭m
B
D♭(♭5)
E♭m
2287
G7
G♭
G+
B♭m
2289
B
D♭(♭5)
E♭m

1st inv.

2291
C♯m
B(♭5)
A
G♯m
2293
F+
E
F7
C♯m
2295
B(♭5)
A
G♯m
F+
2297
E
F7
C♯m

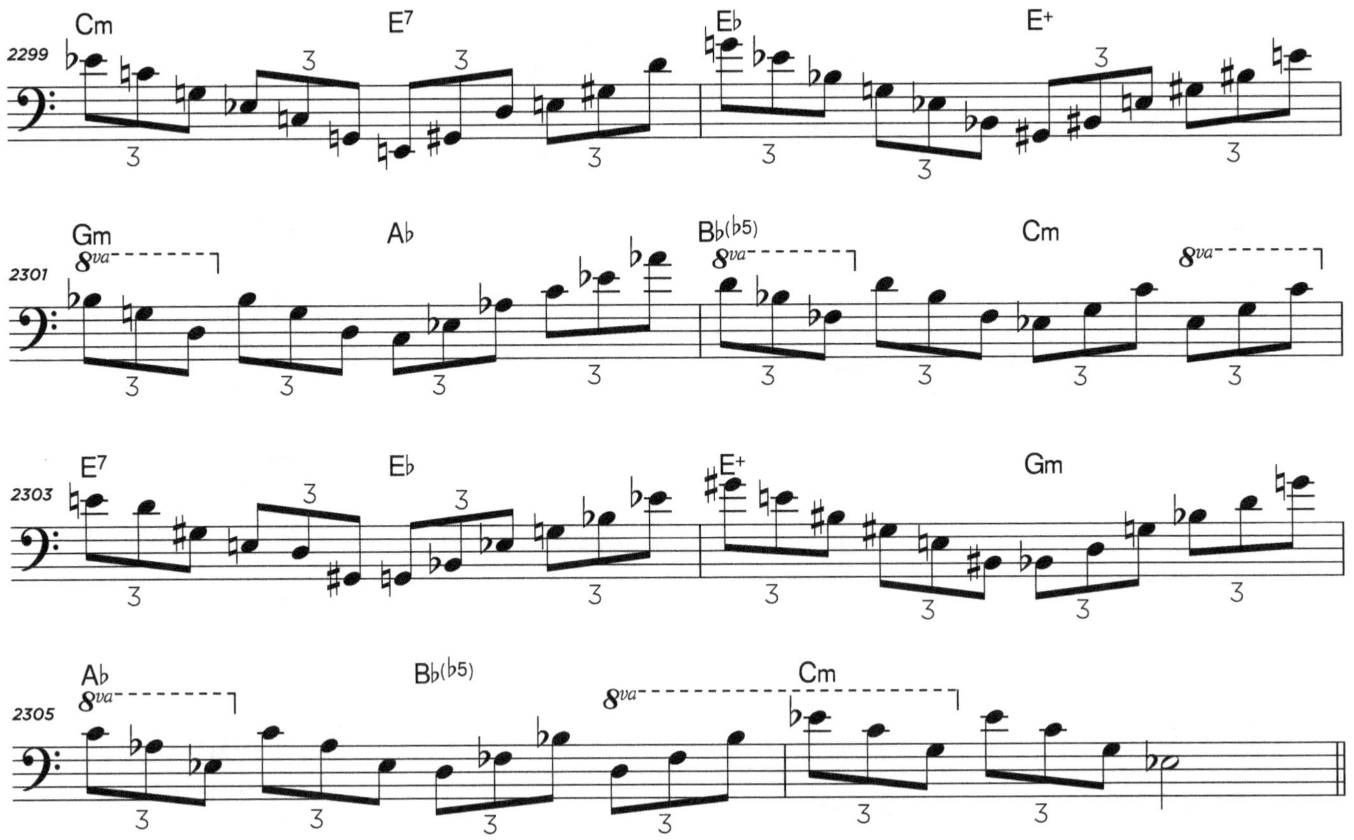
2299
Cm
E7
E♭
E+
2301
Gm
A♭
B♭(♭5)
Cm
2303
E7
E♭
E+
Gm
2305
A♭
B♭(♭5)
Cm

2nd inv.

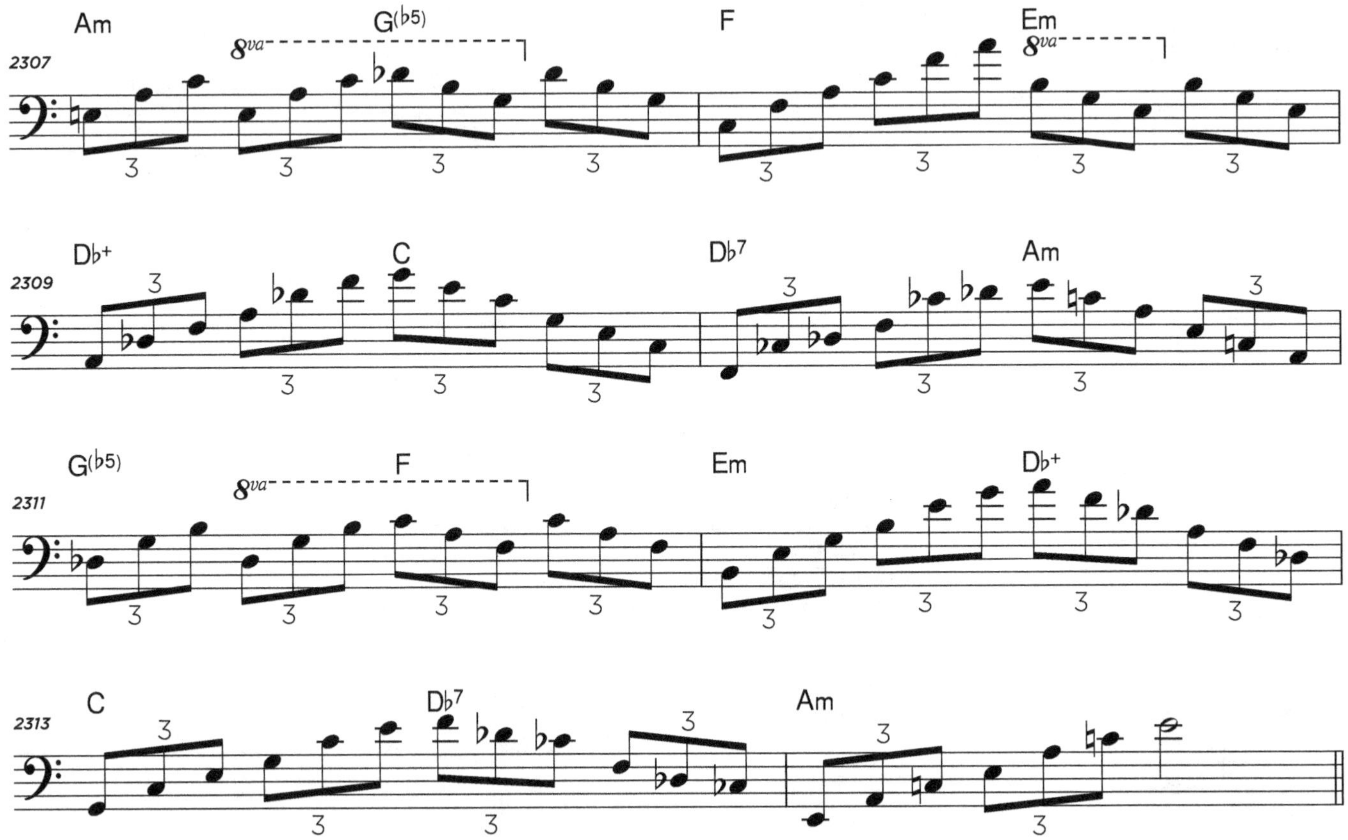
2307
Am
G(♭5)
F
Em
2309
D♭+
C
D♭7
Am
2311
G(♭5)
F
Em
D♭+
2313
C
D♭7
Am

Voice Leading

#37

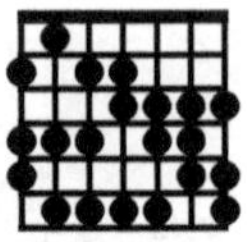

2331 (dh)
(ef)
2333 (li)
(qd)
2335 (he)
(fl)
2337 (iq)
Em F♯(sus2) G C♯m Bm C♯o D(♭5)
Arpeggios
root pos.
2339 Em D(♭5) C♯o Bm
2341 C♯m G F♯(sus2) Em
2343 D(♭5) C♯o Bm C♯m
2345 G F♯(sus2) Em

2347
E♭m
F(sus2)
G♭
Cm
2349
B♭m
C°
D♭(♭5)
E♭m
2351
F(sus2)
G♭
Cm
B♭m
2353
C°
D♭(♭5)
E♭m

1st inv.

2355
C♯m
B(♭5)
A♯°
G♯m
2357
B♭m
E
E♭(sus2)
C♯m
2359
B(♭5)
A♯°
G♯m
B♭m
2361
E
E♭(sus2)
C♯m

2nd inv.

© 2017 by Felix Pastorius

Voice Leading

#38

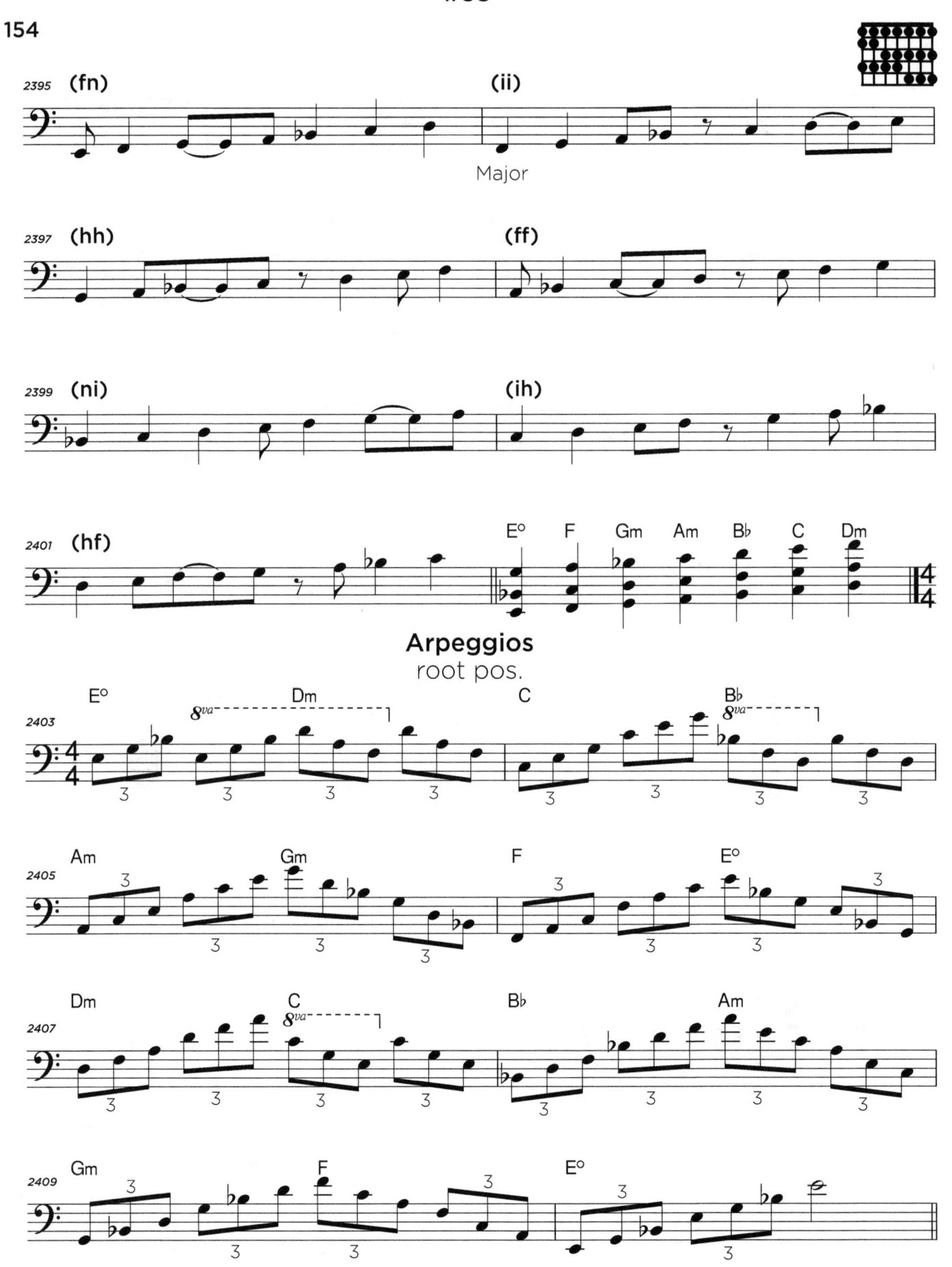

155

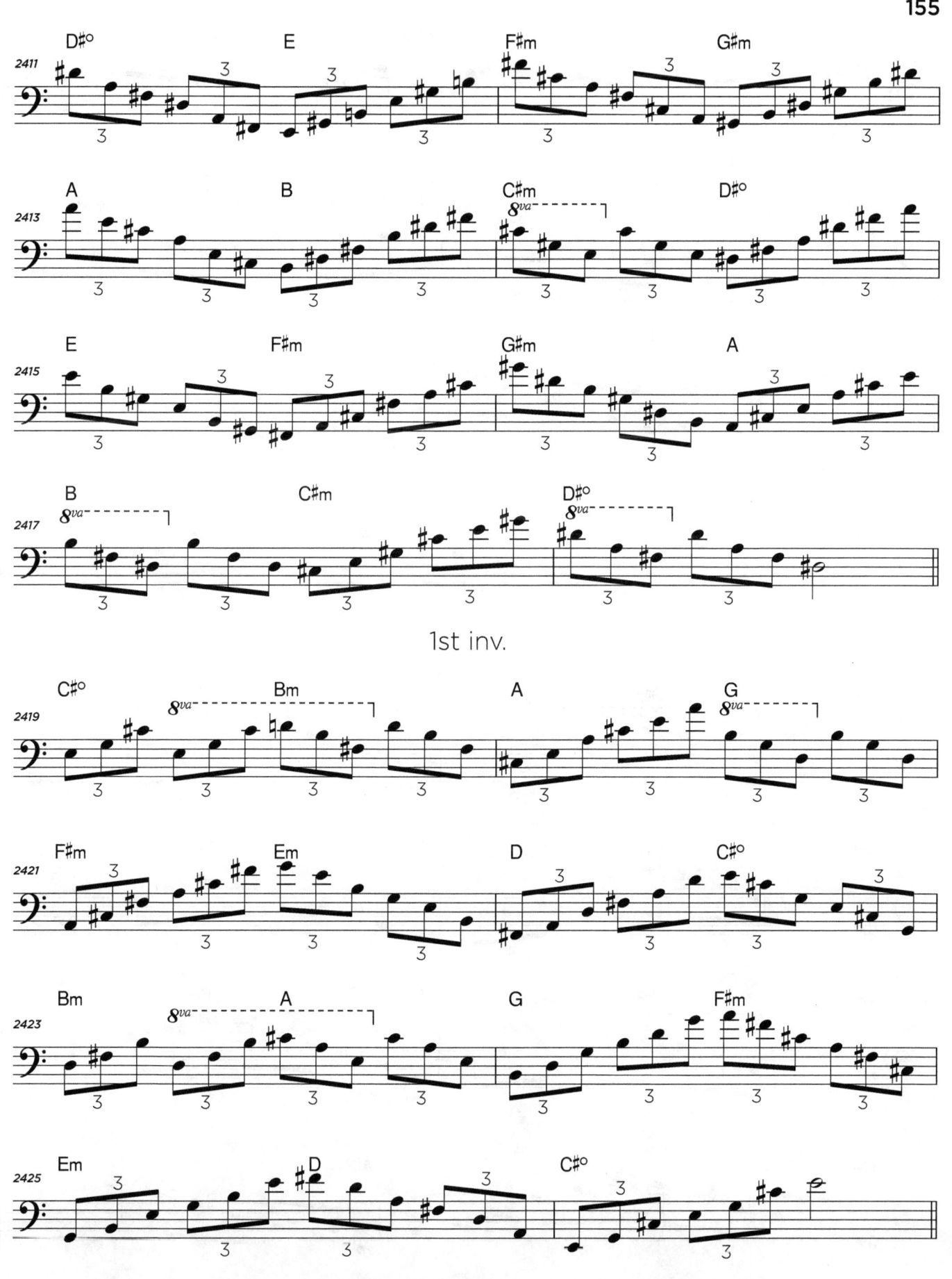

156

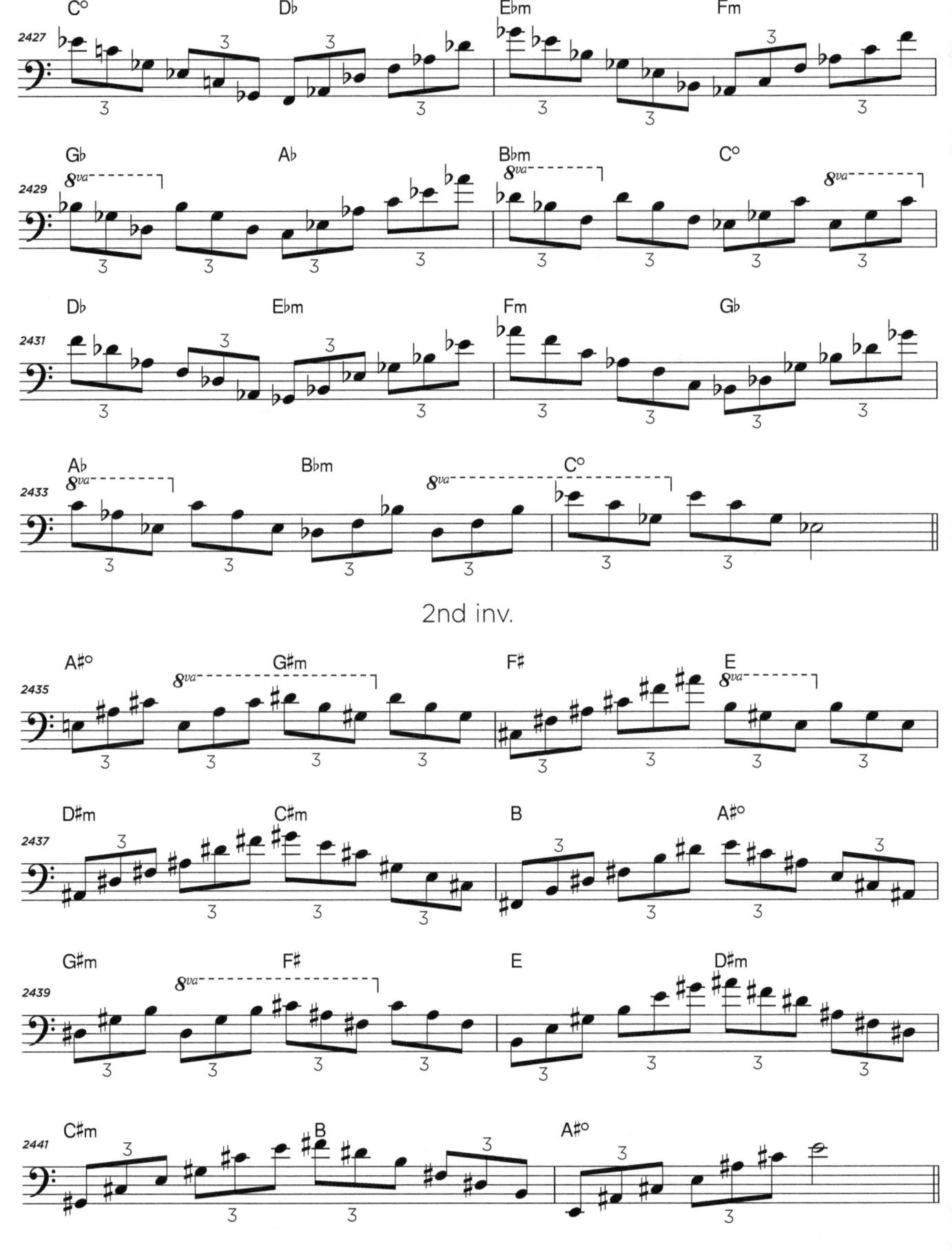

Voice Leading

Breathe

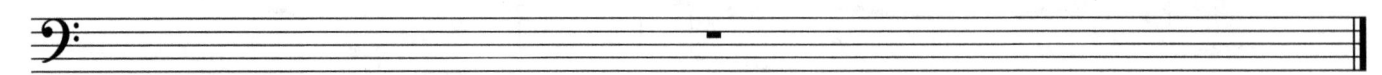

158

2459